A Practical Handbook for
WordPress Themes

A Practical Handbook for
WordPress Themes

By Tristan Denyer

edited by Marci Daniels

A Practical Handbook for WordPress Themes

Tristan Denyer

San Francisco, California, United States

On the web at https://store.tristandenyer.com

To report errors, typos, corrections, send an email to hello@tristandenyer.com.

Corrections can be found at https://store.tristandenyer.com/errata

ISBN-13:   978-1-4997-9708-4

ISBN-10:   1-4997-9708-7

10 9 8 7 6 5 4 3 2 1

Printed by CreateSpace.

Contents

Main content

Appendix

About the Author

Tristan Denyer is a UX designer for web and mobile, front-end web developer, and tech blogger in San Francisco, California. He specializes in HTML, CSS, UX, UI, progressive enhancement (PE), responsive web design (RWD), SEO, WordPress security, and custom WordPress themes.

Over the years he has had the pleasure of working for and with some notable companies and brands, such as New Balance shoes, PF Flyers shoes, Samsung, Hansen Beverage Company, Google Places, Symantec/Norton, Nestlé Professional, Stouffer's, Directly, Walmart.com and others. He is currently the Lead UX Designer at DwellAware.

When he finally shuts the lid on his laptop, he dedicates his free time to being Ozzie's dad, Marci's partner, and to working on small projects that often involve a trip (or five) to the little hardware store down the street.

He can be found in various ways:

Twitter — @tristandenyer

GitHub — https://github.com/tristandenyer

LinkedIn — http://www.linkedin.com/in/tristandenyer

Website and blog — http://tristandenyer.com/

About the Editor

Marci Daniels is a writer living in San Francisco, California. When not writing, or reading other people's writing, she spends her time co-owning and managing the raddest roller skate shop in the world.

Acknowledgements

Writing this book would not have been possible without the numerous clients and agencies that trusted me with their websites over the years.

I would like to thank Jeff Patterson for asking me to be a contributor to Directly, and for doing everything first and making it all less intimidating. Seeing his book *Audio on the Web: The Official IUMA Guide* on a bookshelf was the impetus for writing a book of my own.

A thank you to all the staff and faculty of Southern Illinois University of Edwardsville (SIUE) that worked with me, inspired me, and mentored me. Howard Rambsy, Eileen Joy, Denise DeGarmo, Mike Reinhardt, Elza Ibroscheva, Musonda Kapatamoyo, Lana Hagan, among others, all taught me the value of sharing knowledge.

A very special thank you to my mom, Circe Denyer, for always encouraging me to be a maker, a doer, a builder of things. From a homegrown photography darkroom to backyard biology lessons, and a room full of computer equipment, she always made sure we had the space to learn and explore.

A massive thank you to my wife, Marci Daniels, for asking me to be a part of her life, and for bringing Ozzie into ours. I couldn't think of a better partner in life than one that appreciates and prefers having one amazing pancake to 10 mediocre ones.

How It All Started

My first experience with WordPress was when I was tasked with migrating the content of a blog for a coffee company to their new website's content management system (CMS.) As luck would have it, the new CMS did not accept the export file WordPress offered. So, there I was, copy and pasting text and re-uploading images by hand. Not a fun way to be introduced to WordPress.

At the same time a few friends were asking me to look into their WordPress sites to change the look and feel of them. I had been doing web design and coding static websites for awhile at that point, but WordPress was a whole different animal. So, I read every WordPress tutorial I could find online, tore through a couple books on theme development, and built my own WordPress theme.

Since then, I have designed, coded, updated, managed, mangled, repaired, improved, migrated, secured and consulted on dozens of WordPress powered websites and blogs.

Why I Wrote This Book

Over the years I have written and rewritten the same emails to numerous clients and friends regarding their WordPress sites' themes. I have seen so many people throw good money after bad when it came to purchasing and modifying themes (myself included.) I have also come across some developer's with great insights to better ways of buying, developing and maintaining WordPress themes.

I was writing an email to a friend about her theme when it dawned on me: I've already written this email. A dozen times, I was sure! And that was when I decided that I would write it one more time, then gather it all up into a book for others to reference. I liked the idea of empowering new web designers, agency staff and experienced bloggers alike with information that can help them have better conversations with their developers.

My other reason for writing this book was a little more personal: to explore the dark and dusty corners of WordPress themes that I have only bumped up against. It forced me to conduct a deeper inquiry into how themes actually connect to and work within WordPress far below the surface.

Who Is This Book for?

This book is for those that have a self-hosted WordPress website(s), but some chapters can help those with a site set up on WordPress.com. (If you need clarification about the difference, be sure to read the next chapter!)

Some other people who might benefit from reading this book include:

The agency, the project manager, the intern

I really envisioned a book that would educate the person who is looking for a theme for their client, and/or who is working with a theme marketplace or theme developer. As a developer that worked on WordPress themes, much of my time was spent educating clients on the capabilities, limitations and pitfalls of themes. I like to think that they walked away from those conversations being able to have a better and more informed conversation about WordPress with their clients and other developers. Plus, projects tend to have a higher success rate when you and the developer are speaking and understanding the same language.

The beginner- to intermediate-level WordPress user

WordPress can be very confusing and contradictory at times. (Even the name is confusing in that seemingly every product and service they make is called "WordPress" and all of its various components are often referred to simply as "WordPress.") So, I will try to start each chapter with the basics for someone who has just started using WordPress, then as a chapter moves along it gets deeper into the conceptual foundations of the subject of each chapter. Read as far into the chapter as you are interested in learning. Though some of the deeper knowledge is quite interesting, only you can decide whether or not it's necessary for what you need to do.

Even if you are brand spanking new to WordPress I hope you will get a lot of good info from reading this book end to end.

The web hybrid

This is a term I use for someone who is a web designer that also knows some web development—or vice versa—and is looking to choose and install a theme that won't limit them (too much.) Not every web designer/developer out there has experience with WordPress and how it works. It has its own terminology, taxonomy and way of pulling it all together that is unlike other content management systems. Web designers/ developers may want to read deeper into the chapters.

The enlistee

And let's not forget the person on the team who pulled the short straw and got tasked with "fixing" the WordPress site because the theme is wonky and someone mentioned "getting a new one." You may or may not have much experience with WordPress or the website itself.

Since you came into this under duress with a badly behaving website sitting on your back you may be looking to get just the basics you need to know about themes. The minimum you should read is the next chapter, and then chapters 1, 2, and 3 to get your task started. Chapters 6, 7, and 8 will finish your task. But, I highly recommend the others too since they will give insights on protecting and managing your website.

What to Expect From Reading This Book

By the end of the book I hope you will:

- Be able to spot future pain points in themes by knowing what to look for

- Know what to ask theme developers before buying any theme

- Know how to validate the theme you installed against the developer's claims (and understand the reasons why those don't always line up)

Heaped on top of those primary areas of focus, there will be some guidance on site/ theme maintenance, how a theme integrates with WordPress, how to swap themes out, and some good words on troubleshooting. My great hope is you will also understand that backing up your website(s) will be the single most important thing you can do, because if you don't, we can't be friends. (Seriously, back it up. We'll talk extensively about this in chapter 5.)

No dark paths

Each section will give an introduction to the topic, what it means to the system as a whole, and (where applicable) the pros and cons of the choices we have to make. In some chapters I recommend a service, product or plugin by name. Know I will never recommend anything that I haven't used myself, or don't stand behind. My goal is to get you on solid ground; not send you down a dark path of uncertainty.

Ultimately, this book is written to empower you to make better choices on your own. In the world of WordPress there are thousands and thousands of choices out there from hundreds of sources. Some days it can be easy to get lost, or bamboozled (or even just *feel* bamboozled.)

A better conversation

You can expect a lot of words—it's a book after all. But in the name of full disclosure, I have a tendency to use 15 words where five may do. As this is all based on hundreds of conversations, phone calls and emails I have written over the years on this subject, when I decided to write this book I chose to be a little more descriptive and less cut and dry than what I've seen in other WordPress or web design guides and manuals.

My job as a representative of the web industry is to help you better understand what you are getting yourself into. Not all of it is puppy dogs and ice cream. Some of it is, but hopefully this book will help shine a light on all aspects of themes so that you can have a better conversation with and/or within the WordPress community, a stronger understanding of what you are working on, and the confidence to make the right choices for you or your client.

You can also expect me to use analogies to help explain complex (or bulky) ideas. I love analogies and think when done right can really help speed up the learning curve.

A new vocabulary

Again, projects tend to have a higher success rate when you and the theme developer are speaking and understanding the same language. Our industry has set terms like "website" and "file," and we always know what they are because we really don't have any other common names for them. Then there are terms like slideshow, carousel, slider, slide deck, rotator… they all mean the same thing, but developers the world over cannot agree on one name for them.

I'm going for consistency in this book. I will let you know if there are other names for things so that you can expand your web search when exploring concepts. I will also use terms that the WordPress development community tends to use to help make your conversations and web searches more successful and productive.

At the end of this book you will find a glossary of terms for this book. Glossary definitions in technical manuals tend to be some of the driest, most underwhelming things on the planet. I find great value in learning industry terms, so I tried not to make these too boring.

What's Not in This Book

The short of it is that this is not a "theme development" book. I will not be covering how to design, develop or code your own theme. There are plenty of great books already on the shelves that cover WordPress theme development specifically. This book is what you need to know before, during and after getting a theme from a developer or marketplace, whether it is purchased, downloaded for free or being designed and developed by a freelancer/agency.

While plugins can be an integral part of themes, and I do mention using them, they are outside the scope of this book. Where I need to I will cover the basics, but in-depth plugin discussion will need to happen in another book.

We also won't be going over how to install the WordPress Core on your server. We are focusing on learning WordPress themes as a consumer (owner), maintenance person and someone that has to live with it day in and day out (operators.) Since it is not possible to have a WordPress site without a theme, that's everyone! <-- Ha! Your first lesson of the book.

Before We Get Started

Most people new to WordPress get confused by this, so I'll just get it out of the way:

- WordPress.org makes WordPress that powers WordPress.com, WordPress.org and self-hosted WordPress websites.

- In other words: WordPress makes WordPress that powers your WordPress website that is not hosted on WordPress.

You can see we need to clear up and define 'the three WordPresses' before we can go on.

WordPress.com vs WordPress.org vs WordPress Core

You need to know that there is a fundamental difference between having a website "on WordPress" and having a site "powered by WordPress." I need to be clear about this because parts of this book do NOT apply to websites using the WordPress.com platform.

At the top of the following chapters you should see one or both of these icons: **.COM** **WP** This is to alert you to which WordPress platform the chapter best applies to. Chapters with **.COM** are applicable for those who have a website on the WordPress.com platform, and **WP** is for people who are using the self-hosted WordPress Core (which is really the focus of this book.)

> **CAUTION:** While I label some chapters as being applicable to .COM and WP know that there will be some parts of the chapter that may not apply to both. There will times that you need to be discerning and careful with what newfound knowledge you apply to your .COM website.

WordPress.com .COM

This is the commercial, for-profit, web app side of the WordPress world that is owned and run by Automattic. It allows people to create a website using the WordPress web app based on the WordPress Core (which we'll learn about below.) This is where millions of people host their WordPress websites, and for those using the "freemium" plan the address bar of your browser will read like *yourwebsite.wordpress.com*.

This is NOT what is known as a self-hosted website. With this "dot com" service of WordPress, you are simply borrowing space on the WordPress.com servers and using their web application to control the content of your site.

You are also limited by what you can do with this site. If you are using the WordPress.com freemium version, you are limited to selecting a theme from the WordPress Theme Directory (marketplace) and cannot add plugins.

> **Pay to play.** If you are on WordPress.com and want to customize a theme from the WordPress Themes Directory, you will need to upgrade to the "Business" version (which allows you to customize fonts and add custom CSS), or the "Enterprise" version (which allows you to customize CSS, JavaScript and use fonts from the Typekit library.) See their "Plans" page for more information: http://store.wordpress.com/plans/

WordPress.com users will need to log into their Admin Panel and navigate to the "My Upgrades" screen (Store > My Upgrades.) This is where the "Business" or "Enterprise" upgrade should show, if applied.

Again, this book was originally written for those with self-hosted WordPress sites. But, depending on which WordPress.com upgrade you have, some chapters may be partially applicable or not at all. This is either because it is not a feature of the Basic ("freemium")/Business/Enterprise model or is for other reasons not allowed by WordPress.com.

WordPress.org

This is the community supported side of WordPress. Much of this website is written and maintained by volunteers around the world, much in the same way Wikipedia works. Only here we also have themes and plugins available for download, much the way the ThemeForest marketplace works. So, think of it as a mashup of Wikipedia and ThemeForest (but everything is free to download.)

Its products are

A.   the flagship Open Source piece of software called WordPress (also referred to as the WordPress Core, or WordPress CMS, by some.)

B.   a marketplace for free themes and plugins

C.   a support section for users and developers of the WordPress Core, as well as for the themes and plugins downloaded from WordPress.org.

WordPress.org does not host websites.

WordPress Core/CMS WP

It is called "WordPress Core" (or "WordPress CMS") since it is the core of your website and keeps it from being confused with the company or the service above. This is the flagship piece of software produced and managed by WordPress.org, and maintained with volunteer help from the WordPress community of developers around the world. It is a package of files installed onto your server by you, your developer, or your web host, therefore the community refers to this as "self-hosted WordPress."

For the rest of this book, you will read it as "WordPress." When I write a sentence like "You must update WordPress", or "WordPress handles such and such an action", I am talking about the WordPress Core that you install on your server for your self hosted website, not the company. If I am talking about the WordPress.com or WordPress.org websites, I will write them out as such.

This book is written mainly for those of you self-hosting your WordPress website. But as I mentioned above, those of you on the WordPress.com platform can use some of the information across these chapters. Hopefully the rest of the information will entice you to move your site to a self-hosted platform so you can take full control.

> **Still Not Clear? Let WordPress explain it better.** Visit http://en.support.wordpress.com/com-vs-org/ to see a side-by-side comparison of hosting your site on WordPress.com versus self-hosting.

Which Do I Have?

In order to understand if this entire book or only parts of it apply to your situation, you need to figure out if you are on WordPress.com or self-hosted. Again, these situations are different in many ways.

If you have no idea where your site is hosted, try the following steps to help figure it out:

- (Best way) Log into your website and look at the address bar in the browser. Does it end in "wordpress.com," such as yourwebsite.wordpress.com? Even if your website is using the Custom Domain service with WordPress.com, your Admin Panel will show yourwebsite.wordpress.com/wp-admin/ in the address bar.

- (If you can't log in) Look at the URL for your website. Does it end in "wordpress.com," such as example.wordpress.com? This is not always definitive of you being on a self-hosted platform since you can pay WordPress.com to mask the URL to show a custom URL you own.

- (If you still have no idea) Look to see who you are paying each month/year. If it is WordPress.com, you are on the **.COM** platform. If it's a hosting company like GoDaddy, HostGator, or WP Engine, you are self-hosted, **WP**.

I hope one of the above helped you figure it out, because you really need to know where your website is hosted—and not just for the sake of this book.

Basic Knowledge Expected

Since this book is discussing themes—which are technically a component of WordPress—I expect that you have a basic understanding of what WordPress is and how to use it. This is important because I will be directing you to the Admin Panel on a regular basis. If this is your first exposure to WordPress, you may find the learning curve a little steeper since you will be learning the Admin Panel at the same time.

The Admin Panel (or administration screens)

The Support pages on WordPress.org call the backend of the WordPress website "Administration Screens." I have yet to meet anyone that calls it that, instead I see

"Admin Panel" or just "Admin", or even "Dashboard" more often than anything else.

Problem with "Dashboard" is that there is a section of the Admin Panel that is labeled "Dashboard", and I have seen some confusion in the WordPress Support pages about that. So, I prefer Admin Panel to describe the part of your WordPress installation that you log into, and each subsection of it are "screens" by which you navigate using the left side menu bar.

You should be able to log into the Admin Panel, and have knowledge of the left side menu bar. For this book we will mainly be accessing the Appearance tab, but some lessons may extend to other tabs.

There is a fairly standard convention used for writing out directions on how to navigate a website. It will often look something like this:

Appearance > Themes > Add New button

It's a breadcrumb style instruction that is short for "Click on Appearance, then click on Themes, then click on the button labeled Add New." In most cases it is also hierarchical (hence the greater-than signs) in that Appearance is the parent of Themes which is the parent of the Install Themes tab. In this book, I will be using this breadcrumb style instruction to direct you around the Admin Panel using the left side menu bar.

Roles

You should have a knowledge of Roles in WordPress, specifically that the "Administrator" is the only one that can install, switch, edit and update themes. You can read more about roles here: http://codex.wordpress.org/Roles_and_Capabilities

If you are not an Administrator of a WordPress site, you will likely have problems following along with this book.

Web host

You should have a basic understanding of what a web host is, and you should know how to log into your web host control panel, or cPanel. The cPanel is where you can also access the files of the WordPress Core—and your theme.

It's possible that you have owned and managed a self-hosted WordPress website without ever having to log into the cPanel. That said, some of the lessons in this book cover advanced (or manual) aspects of themes that have the option for you to manage your theme(s) via the cPanel. One such task where I recommend logging into the cPanel comes up in chapter 10 when we inventory your themes and look for sneaky ones that got installed but don't register in the Admin Panel.

Master web developer

Just kidding: you don't need to know anything about coding to research, buy, install and/or manage themes. It certainly helps to know how to code because you will have a deeper understanding of how all the pieces of a theme work together. But the point of this book is to teach you pretty much everything but the code so that you can have a better conversation with WordPress theme developers.

That brings us to our next chapter where I will introduce you to what a theme is and what it controls.

Introduction to Themes:
Principle Concept

What Is a Theme?

The technical answer is that the theme is the display layer of the website: what you see on on the page when you visit your site is styled and presented by your theme's files. Those files can be as little as two, or in some cases, hundreds of files.

Theme files are made up of code: PHP, HTML, and CSS, but can also (and often do) include images, JavaScript, APIs, fonts, plugins, and more. Don't worry about these terms just yet; though it's the latter part that should concern you greatly when choosing a theme, and we'll get into that in chapter 3.

> **The WordPress Codex states:** *"Fundamentally, the WordPress Theme system is a way to 'skin' your weblog. Yet, it is more than just a 'skin.' Skinning your site implies that only the design is changed. WordPress Themes can provide much more control over the look and presentation of the material on your website."* (source: http://codex.wordpress.org/Using_Themes)

So a theme does control things like how blog posts will appear on the homepage, but it also offers control over various ways the blog will be viewed or function. For instance, over things like whether you want to show who wrote a blog post or not, how many comments are on each post, and whether you want the text be black under a blue header or some other color, to name a few. WordPress themes have many dynamic areas that get filled with information from your database (text and images), third-parties (Twitter), and your users' interactions with the site (comments.)

Analogy for a WordPress theme

Those that know me have heard this 'house analogy' plenty of times when it comes to talking about websites, and I believe it is particularly good at describing how WordPress (and other content management systems) works.

Your WordPress website is made up four parts: the Core, the Theme, the Content, and the Database. For this analogy think of:

- **the Core** as the basic structure of a house (foundation, outer walls, plumbing, wiring, roof);

- **the Theme** as the finish work of the house (flooring, paint, faucets, electrical sockets, and even the interior walls that are not load bearing—meaning holding the roof up);

- **the Content** is your stuff (furniture, pictures, throw rugs, and shelves);

- **the Database** is the detailed map and inventory of the contents (*where* your stuff is located in the house, the attributes like color, and *how much* of it there is).

> **The more you know.** The Theme lives inside the Core, and much of the Content lives inside the Database. Though technically uploaded images, documents and video live in a folder outside the Database, the Database knows where to find them.

If you were to move the couch (Content) to the other side of the room, you would be updating the details (Database) of your house. Just as if you changed a word on a blog post your Database gets updated with the change. The structure part of WordPress does not change, just as moving a couch or adding a throw rug does not change the overall structure of your house.

In regards to switching or modifying themes, we could think of switching to a new theme as doing a heavy remodel to your house (covered in chapter 12), or modifying your existing theme as doing some painting or a light remodel of your home (covered in chapter 12.)

An Educated Choice

So, a theme is a skin that controls what your website's visitors view and interact with on your site. It can also limit and expand the amount and type of content they can see. For example, a certain theme might show only three blog posts on the home page, whereas another shows 10. Or, a theme could have the ability to show thumbnails of featured images with the blog post excerpt. Maybe on one theme a Twitter feed comes built in, and on other themes it does not. The point is that myriad solutions are possible. It is up to the developer to decide which features are necessary for a given theme.

One of the missions of this book is to discuss how you can be critical of these solutions and be able to make educated choices when you select a theme for your WordPress powered website. Selecting a WordPress theme is a lot like selecting a car: you have needs (seats four), wants (sunroof) and distractions (spinning rims). Spend too much time with the distractions and you might forget that your family of four won't fit in that two-seater.

What Are Parent and Child Themes?

One way to modify a theme is to edit the files of the theme. Another way is to add to (or override) its functionality and styles with another theme. Modifying theme files is not optimal because you can no longer install updates for the theme. The second way, using a method called Child themes, is better. This is preferred because you can modify your Parent theme and still get updates for the Parent theme while any modifications made by the Child theme remain in place.

> **Modifying themes.** In chapter 11 we will discuss more about the principles of modifying a theme that explain why you don't want to make modifications to the theme files if you plan on installing theme updates.

A Parent-Child theme setup is having two separate themes that work in tandem. The way it works is, say you install and activate a theme, and later on you find that it is missing some functionality like an expanded footer, or you want to add another page template. You would be able do this by installing and activating a Child theme that specifically gives you a new footer or page template.

The Parent theme often does the bulk of the work, but the Child theme comes in and adds, removes or modifies specific parts of the Parent theme. Together their output works as one. If you remove the Child theme, the Parent theme remains intact and any changes made by the Child theme are gone.

> **Caution:** Adding a Child theme to a Parent theme can move your widgets to the "Inactive Widgets" area of the Appearance > Widgets screen. Meaning, they will need to be added back by dragging them into the the appropriate widget areas. The placement of widgets in the widgets areas is tied to the theme that is active. Once you apply the same widgets to Parent and Child, you can freely switch between the two since the database will remember the place and contents of widgets for each specific theme.

Where Do Themes Come From?

Themes mostly come from web developers since they require knowledge of PHP, HTML and CSS (at the very least.) *Mostly?* I say that because some web designers are also getting into the theme market. Some developers can also design the look and feel of a theme, while some designers can also write code. In some cases a designer and a developer will collaborate on a theme.

WordPress.org does not develop themes outside the small collection of "default" themes that have come with the WordPress versions over the years. And WordPress does not require themes to be submitted to them for their approval and release. Today, themes are developed by anyone that wants to create one, including freelancers, web designers, agencies, and students.

Anyone with access to the internet can write and share (or sell) a theme to anyone. Theme developers can choose to submit it to the WordPress Themes Directory (which at time of this writing has 2,603 themes available for download) or they can distribute it on their own.

> **Where does support come from?** Keep in mind that just because the theme came from the WordPress Themes Directory does not mean WordPress.org supports it —themes are simply "subject to review" by WordPress Theme Review Team (see details of the review process: http://codex.wordpress.org/Theme_Review). Support comes from the developer that uploaded the theme, not WordPress.org.

Due to the popularity of WordPress today, it has spurred a worldwide industry in theme development. Some companies do nothing but develop and sell themes, while others have added it to their list of services. Whereas companies like Envato's

ThemeForest simply provide a marketplace for themes and rely on developers to create, submit and support the themes in the marketplace.

> **CAUTION:** Be aware that if you choose to install WordPress via your web hosting cPanel, then, depending on your web host, you may find that numerous themes come with the initial installation. I once witnessed a major web host load over 30 themes with my initial installation of WordPress.
>
> Regina Smola of WPSecurityLock.com used DreamHost's "One-Click Install" for a new WordPress installation and found it downloaded 134 themes, some with security vulnerabilities! (source: http://www.wpsecuritylock.com/dreamhost-one-click-wordpress-installed-timthumb-vulnerability-and-security-risks/)
>
> See chapter 13 where I cover uninstalling/deleting unwanted themes.

Why Are Themes Important?

Well, they're not so "important" as they are mandatory—your WordPress website will not work unless you have at least one theme installed. At the time of this writing, WordPress 3.9 installs with three themes: "Twenty Fourteen" and "Twenty Thirteen" and "Twenty Twelve." The "Twenty Fourteen" theme is the default theme for 3.9, and I highly recommended that you leave it installed.

I'll go into this more in depth later in this book, but know you should only have 2 to 3 themes installed at a time, with 2 being optimal. One theme will be the one you are using, and the other is a backup. To go one further, I highly recommend you always use the default theme for the current version of WordPress as the backup.

The default themes are designed and developed by WordPress.org and the WordPress community of developers that volunteer their time to work on it, fix bugs and make it production-ready. Since WordPress is free, so are these themes, as well as the previous default themes "Twenty Eleven", "Twenty Ten", "Classic" and the original "Kubrick" theme.

Default theme as backup. Keeping the default theme installed as a backup theme is a smart move for two reasons. One is that if your active theme is accidentally deleted from the server or WordPress declares it "broken," it will automatically activate the default theme for that version of WordPress. It's also good to have around so you can switch to it if your active theme starts to give you major problems.

The default theme for WordPress 3.8 and 3.9 is "Twenty Fourteen", WordPress 3.6 through 3.7 is "Twenty Thirteen", and 3.2 through 3.5 uses "Twenty Twelve". WordPress will only activate them if they are already installed and their folder names have not been altered.

Introduction to Themes:
Anatomy of a Theme

In the previous chapter we went over the principles of a theme and used the 'house analogy' that labeled themes as "the finish work of the house." Let's get into what those pieces and parts are that make up a theme.

Anatomy of a Theme

Not all themes are coded or designed or even function the same. But there are some elements that are mandatory to a theme in order for it to be recognized by your installation of WordPress as a "valid" theme. And then there are some elements that are not mandatory, but that are common to most themes today.

It's up to the theme developer

You can think of each .php file of a theme as an enabler. By that I mean WordPress has hundreds of things available to developers such as actions, filters, functions, APIs, loops, hooks and more. If a developer does not put in a specific function to do something like enabling Featured Images to show on Posts, then they won't show (even if you assign a featured image to a Post.) Themes do not come with all possible functions and features of WordPress; each one is enabled by a developer adding its code to the theme.

When a developer decides to use a function such as Featured Images, they also need to decide parameters like size of the image, if it should link to the Post or to the image itself, alt tags, and how it aligns on the page (left, center, right.) And Featured Images is just one possible function of a theme! There are literally hundreds of these pieces and

7

parts that developers have at their disposal, each with their own set of parameters.

> **Analogy:** In the previous chapter we compared WordPress Core to the structure of a house. We mentioned that wiring should be considered embedded in the structure. This wiring reaches every part of the house. The theme is like the finish work, which would include electrical sockets.
>
> These electrical sockets can be thought of as the actions, filters, functions, APIs, loops, and hooks of a theme. The electricity is available in the wall, but if the contractor did not put in an electrical socket on a wall, you don't have the ability to tap into that power. In fact, you would have to tear open the wall and add an outlet, just like you would need a developer to modify the theme (see chapter 11.)

The mandatory parts of a theme

While WordPress.org does not dictate how themes must be made, they do have a short list of items that must be present in order for WordPress Core to consider it a valid theme and allow it to be activated. In fact, it's only two files: the style.css file for styling the website's overall look and feel; and the index.php that basically gathers any other files for the theme.

> **WordPress Codex.** Again: WordPress.org does not dictate how themes must be made, but they do however manage a space called the Codex where developers, owners and operators can share and find the latest guidance on theme development. While it can get very technical at times, it's not just for developers: http://codex.wordpress.org/

When you upload a theme to WordPress via the Admin Panel, it unzips the file and looks for the style.css mainly to get the name and version of the theme from the topmost part of the file called the stylesheet header. Frankly, WordPress doesn't care if there is any code (or CSS rules) beyond this, though if it didn't your site would look pretty sparse.

WordPress uses this stylesheet header to identify the theme, as well as index it in the "Themes" section (Appearance > Themes) and to display supporting details about it.

```
/*
Theme Name: Twenty Thirteen
Theme URI: http://wordpress.org/themes/twentythirteen
Author: the WordPress team
Author URI: http://wordpress.org/
Description: The 2013 theme for WordPress takes us back to the blog, featuring a full range of post
formats, each displayed beautifully in their own unique way. Design details abound, starting with a
vibrant color scheme and matching header images, beautiful typography and icons, and a flexible layout
that looks great on any device, big or small.
Version: 1.0
License: GNU General Public License v2 or later
License URI: http://www.gnu.org/licenses/gpl-2.0.html
Tags: black, brown, orange, tan, white, yellow, light, one-column, two-columns, right-sidebar, flexible-
width, custom-header, custom-menu, editor-style, featured-images, microformats, post-formats, rtl-
language-support, sticky-post, translation-ready
Text Domain: twentythirteen

This theme, like WordPress, is licensed under the GPL.
Use it to make something cool, have fun, and share what you've learned with others.
*/
```

A screen capture of a valid CSS header for the default theme "Twenty Thirteen."

It also looks for the index.php file which has two basic jobs: one is to gather up any other theme files it needs to build the structure of the site, and the other is to make a request to the database for content to show on the page. This content could be things like blog posts, page content, and widgets, as well as build the navigation menu. In many themes, this file also builds the home page.

Another mandatory part of a theme is really a piece of code within a file, and it's called "the loop." It's a complex and powerful piece of code that talks with the database to get things like a list of blog posts, content for Posts and Pages, as well as all the common elements like the title, metadata, excerpts, tags and more. You will often find a loop on a handful of files in your theme.

> **The Loop.** WordPress doesn't care if the loop is in your index.php file, or any other file for that matter. It doesn't even look for it when you upload the theme. But, it is a mandatory part of the theme for the fact that you need it to get dynamic content from your database. And for that reason, themes have at least one loop installed. Further reading on the loop: http://codex.wordpress.org/The_Loop_in_Action

Common pieces of a theme

There are some elements that you can count on to be in the vast majority of well-coded themes. For instance, the header, footer, sidebars and navigation are in almost every theme. They may look different and live in different parts of the screen for each theme, but they are there.

> **Buying tip:** When looking for a theme, look for the terms "sidebar", or better yet, "widgetized sidebar" (which I'll explain below.) There is a trend toward dropping the two-column layout in favor of a full-width layout in order to 'clean it up.' I'm not fully convinced this is a good layout to rely on for your entire website, so I recommend you buy a theme with the traditional two-column plus sidebar option still available.

Since WordPress started out as a blogging platform, themes that want to use Pages to make their site more like a traditional website (not just a blog) will need a page.php file. This file controls the content for a Page, such as its structure and layout, title, metadata, the main content, whether it has a sidebar or not, and more. Today, it is pretty rare for a theme to not have a page.php file.

The sister file to page.php is the single.php file. It displays your individual Posts. Where the index.php file can be used to show what some refer to as the "blog roll" (a list of all your Posts), the single.php file shows only one of those posts. It too dictates things like structure and layout, title, metadata, the main content, whether it has a sidebar or not, and on and on.

When visitors view pages for archives, categories or tags, the theme uses the index.php file. The developer can control the content and layout of these sections using an archive.php, category.php, and tag.php file, respectively.

A theme without sidebars is like a house without windows. Sidebars allow you to dynamically showcase just about any content you have on your site in a specific area of the page, which is why many themes will come with at least one or two sidebars. You may see them showing lists of Pages, Recent Posts, tags clouds, Twitter feeds and more.

Crazy as it sounds, while navigation menus are very common to websites, being able to customize them in the Admin Panel is not always possible. You would think this would be mandatory, but the fact is allowing a user to customize the order and names of tabs in the navigation menu is something a developer has to include in the theme's functions.php file. So keep that in mind when selecting a theme.

Names

All themes have a name attributed to them. You will find themes called "Twenty Thirteen," "Solo," "Canvas," "Ozzie" and on and on. In a world where there are tens of thousands of themes floating around and no global WordPress theme name registry, you could come across two or even six themes with the same name. This can be confusing for those times where you are searching for a theme based on the name *you* know it by.

Public themes found in marketplaces use this name (much like any other product does) to brand it apart from others and make it memorable. Custom themes created for one client will have a name attributed to it because WordPress requires it to have one, and that name can be anything (I once saw a custom theme called "Magic Johnson" and another called "onetwothreefour.")

> **There can be only one.** Theme names and their respective folders play an important role when you go to install your theme, or go to add another theme to your website. In chapter 6 we will go over what names—especially folder names—mean for themes.
>
> For now, know that you can only have one theme folder named "awesometheme." If you were to find another theme developer selling a different theme also called "Awesome Theme", it is highly likely that its folder name would be "awesometheme" as well. And this will become problematic when you go to install it. Again, more on this in chapter 6.

Widgets, and widgetizing

The WordPress Admin Panel has the capability built into it to control the placement and content of widgets. During the coding of a theme, a developer must consider if it will be "widgetized", how many widgetized areas there will be, and where they will be placed on the page as well as any specific styling for them. Most developers have at least one to three widgetized areas made available.

Contrary to popular belief, they do not have to be in a sidebar. They can be located just about anywhere on the page: in the header, before the footer, in the footer, across the middle of a home page, and even assigned to Custom Post Types.

It is important to know that widgetized areas are tied to the theme. Meaning, if your current theme has three widget areas in the footer, it's likely your new theme won't recognize them, even if it too has three areas for widgets in the footer. The reason is that the theme's widgets have unique names assigned to them and each of them is coded differently. It is highly unlikely that your new theme will have the exact same names and code for its widget areas.

See chapter 12 for more of what to expect when switching themes.

Screen capture showing inactive widgets. This can happen when you switch to a new theme that does not recognize the previous theme's unique widget names and structure. All information and settings in the widgets is saved.

The Theme Package: Contents

Theme packages are .zip files that include:

a) theme files (.php, .css, .js, .jpg, .txt, etc.)

b) sometimes secondary files like dummy content, plugins and documentation

c) tertiary assets like Photoshop files (more common with ThemeForest downloads)

d) and even non-related items like hidden system files, and markdown files meant for GitHub.

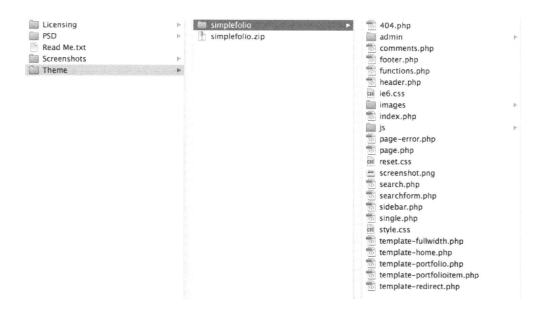

A screen capture showing the contents of a typical theme package. In this example, you would upload the "simplefolio.zip" file. We'll go over this in detail in chapter 6.

Theme files

We already introduced you to these, and will cover them again throughout the book.

Photoshop files

Photoshop files (files ending in .psd) are technically not part of the theme, though some marketplaces like ThemeForest will deliver them with the theme download package. These files are there to help you if you ever need to create new image assets like backgrounds or other visual treatments.

You should not upload Photoshop files to your server because they are often large files (further burdening your backup process,) and are not needed by the theme. If you want to keep them, store them locally (on your laptop.)

Dummy content (or sample content)

Some theme developers include an .xml file that contains dummy content (sample Posts and Pages with text and images.) If you are starting a site from scratch, you may find that this dummy content is helpful to flesh out the site a bit and speed up the initial setup. One benefit is that some themes come with numerous shortcodes, and these dummy content files often add a page called "shortcodes" to help show you how they work (though shortcodes can sometimes be found in the documentation or marketing pages.)

> **Caution:** If you have an existing website and are switching themes DO NOT import this dummy content. Your existing website already has content, so it can cause confusion by adding more Pages and Posts to your website.

This content can be imported to your website via the Tools > Import screen in the Admin Panel (self-hosted users will be prompted to install the WordPress Importer plugin.) This content is often similar to the content you see in the demo found on the theme's marketing pages, and usually contains some Pages, Posts, menu items, main content and images.

I find the vast majority of this content to be counter-productive, and in some cases the imported dummy content can be forgotten and turn into odd pages your visitors (or Google) may stumble across. Before you go live you will have to comb through your Posts and Pages to make sure all dummy content is removed, or hidden by placing into draft mode if you want to keep it.

> **Skip it.** I recommend not using the dummy content. This file is really for people setting up theme demonstrations. If you have a client and you feel uncomfortable sending them to the theme developer's demo to see how it works, only then would you use this dummy content to quickly create your own demo website.

Documentation / instructions

You may see a folder in the .zip file you downloaded from a marketplace or developer that says something like "docs", "instructions" or "read me." These are either PDF or HTML files that help you with setting up your theme and other related details.

I highly recommend you always read through the documentation before you upload your theme. If you ever have an issue with setting up a theme, make sure you refer to the documentation before you contact the developer. Read twice, set up once, as they say.

I recommend not uploading these to your server. In the vast majority of cases, they can run locally (off your laptop or USB drive.) Even if you are installing this for a client, I recommend keeping all documentation/instructions off the server and simply sending them to the client to store locally. Why? If you store these files in the theme folder, or in the WordPress Core, they could be lost during the next Theme or Core update. If you must, store them in a folder at the root level of your server (outside WordPress.)

I believe all purchased themes (even custom themes where you hired a developer to create it) should include documentation with the download. It doesn't have to be a 200-page book, but it should cover step-by-step documentation of all features that are controlled by the theme, like sliders, galleries, shortcodes, forums and online storefronts, and instructions on how to use them. High fives for the developers that go so far as to have links to video tutorials for complex features!

No docs from WordPress Theme Directory. Don't expect extensive documentation from themes downloaded from the WordPress Theme Directory. In most cases there is a "readme.txt" file included in the download that documents the basic feature set of the theme.

If you install your theme directly from the WordPress Theme Directory using the Appearance > Themes > Add New button, then you will not see the download files, nor the readme.txt file. You can, however, view the readme in the three following ways:

- View in the browser by visiting: yourwebsite.com/wp-content/themes/ themefoldername/readme.txt You will need to change out the domain name for yours and the theme name for the theme you installed (this is typically all lowercase and one word.)

- View on the server via your web host's cPanel.

- Go to the Directory (http://wordpress.org/themes/) and search for the theme and download the files to your computer.

Plugins

Some theme downloads from marketplaces come with a folder containing third-party plugins. These can be for building forms, sliders, video galleries, and more. You will need to refer to the documentation or marketing pages to see if these plugins are required or recommended (see chapter 9, "Dealing with the required and recommended plugins for themes," which also covers bait and switch and other gray-area business practices.)

Plugins do not get uploaded with a theme. They are uploaded using the Plugins > Add

New screen.

Superfluous files

You may find non-related items like system-specific files (Mac OSX .dstore files) or GitHub files (usually .md and .gitignore files.) These are typically harmless when uploaded with a theme, though if you run the plugin "Theme-Check," you may see a recommendation to remove them.

Worse-case scenarios are themes with malware, viruses and other malicious crap. For theme packages that I download, I always scan them with my anti-virus program to check for malware *before* I upload it to my server. If malware exists, I delete the entire theme package from my computer and notify the developer and or marketplace.

Once a theme is activated, I run Theme-Check to verify the contents and "test for compliance with the [WordPress.org marketplace] Theme Review guidelines." If I find any major issues with Theme-Check, I notify the developer. I may still use the theme depending on the number and severity of the issues, but major ones may make me think twice.

Marketplace theme validation. Some marketplaces have a set of rules and minimum standards by which they test and validate themes and theme packages submitted to them. This can include the way the theme is structured, certain theme options, files included in the download (Photoshop files, documentation, images, etc), as well as ensuring HTML and CSS is valid. But, in no way does it mean all of this applies for all vendors. Some don't check at all.

Check with the marketplace for a list of standards developers must meet. A vague list or no mention of standards/checks may be a sign for you to stay away from that marketplace. A long, prescriptive set of features and options themes "must have" is also a sign of a marketplace directing the market, and not allowing the developers, designers and customers to work that out for themselves.

An example of a list of standards is ThemeForest's "WordPress Theme Submission Requirements": http://support.envato.com/index.php?/Knowledgebase/Article/View/472 (Included here without comment.)

The Theme Package: Source

There are three sources for theme packages:

1)   WordPres.org using the in-app method (Admin Panel) or the manual method

2)   download from marketplace, agency or developer

3)   and the one you created. Yes, you too can create a theme package. There is nothing proprietary or secretive about it: you just compress the theme files into a .zip file. Chapter 6 will go into detail about the format and structure of the contents of a .zip file.

Download and install from WordPress.org

This is considered the most lightweight option in that it only installs the necessary theme files and nothing else. Downloading from WordPress.org can happen two ways: in-app and manual.

The in-app method is done by logging in to your Admin Panel. Self-hosted sites require you to navigate to the Appearance > Themes > Add New screen. WordPress.com sites require you to navigate to the Appearance > Themes screen to start browsing.

In the case of the self-hosted site, you are searching for a theme in the WordPress.org marketplace and installing it (add it to your server) by clicking on the "Install now" ink. In the case of the WordPress.com sites, you are searching for a theme in the WordPress.org marketplace and activating it by clicking on the "Activate" ink. We'll go over the differences of installing and activating in later chapters. The key takeaway here is that self-hosted sites store the theme files on their server. WordPress.com sites all share the same centralized theme files.

The manual method for installing themes from WordPress.org is only for self-hosted sites. It requires you to visit the http://wordpress.org/themes/ marketplace, download a theme package to your computer, then upload it to your self-hosted WordPress installation (see chapter 6, for details on the three ways to install a downloaded theme.) Again, every download I have received from WordPress.org only delivers the necessary theme files—no/minimal documentation, no Photoshop files, no junk.

Download from a marketplace or developer

This is considered the most full-featured option in that it often includes documentation, instructions, and sometimes Photoshop files and suggested plugins. In fact, downloading from a marketplace or developer can be interesting and surprising in what you get in the theme package. It can be anything from simply just the theme files, to a 'grab bag' collection of folders and files that make you question what they have to do with the theme at all.

Over the years I have found the following files in my theme downloads: a few .mp3 songs from an unknown metal band, malware, plugins, a .zip file with hundreds of low-quality stock photography images still with watermarks, other themes by the developer, and I even once got a dummy content file that was chock full of links to veterinary pharmaceutical sites.

Introduction to Themes:
Types of Themes

In the previous chapter we went over the anatomy of a theme and dove into what you can expect in a theme package. For this chapter, we'll get into the types of themes that are out there, and get an introduction to the pros and cons of each of these types.

Types of Themes

Themes can be broken down into four types:

- purchased (or "premium")

- free (including "freemium")

- boilerplate (starter/developer theme)

- full-custom

These "types" should not to be confused with the numerous categories that are used to help group themes based on design or function (e.g., ecommerce, corporate, nonprofit, magazine) which you will use when looking through a theme marketplace.

Why does knowing the types matter?

Understanding the types of themes helps you find the theme that will best suit your needs, and in some cases it will also help you decide where to look. Such as:

- If you are looking for a theme that you can download today and that often comes with customer support, then you are likely looking to purchase a theme (or join a theme "club.")

- If saving money is the highest priority, then you may be looking for a free theme. (Note: Some developers also offer a "lite" version of their premium themes for free, and this can be a great way to test drive the theme before you buy the full-featured version.)

- If you are a developer or designer—with knowledge of coding, or are learning how to code—and want a jumpstart on developing a new theme, you are likely looking for a Boilerplate or Starter theme.

- If you are looking for a theme with a custom design and layout that is not being used by anyone else, and/or require some custom features, you are looking for a Full-custom theme.

The following four sections will cover each type in detail. The next couple chapters will explain where to buy, find, and order themes, as well as how to buy the right theme for you.

Is one better than the other?

Yes. I will go over some pros and cons for each type in chapter 3. But ultimately, only you can decide which type is best suited for your needs.

Purchased Themes

Also called "Premium" themes, purchased themes are just that: themes you purchase from an online vendor for a one-time fee, or in some cases an annual fee (also called a Theme Club.) That vendor can be a freelancer, agency, or business with an online marketplace, though many (if not most) commercial themes created today are designed and developed by a single person.

These themes often come with free updates, documentation/instructions, dummy content to get you started (e.g., Posts, Pages, images), and support for when things go wonky. In some cases, there are video tutorials, support forums, and Photoshop files for the theme. Increasingly these types of themes also include plugins in the download, or include a list of mandatory and recommended plugins to use with the theme.

Support for these types of themes is varied. In the case of Elegant Themes, you must pay a yearly fee for their "Premium Technical Support", whereas ThemeForest support is free from the theme's developer. Elsewhere, I have seen a tiered support offered where you can pay more for faster service. One company, YIThemes, requires you to activate your theme to get access to the support forum (http://yithemes.com/theme-activation/).

> **No images.** Keep in mind that the photos you see in the demos/previews often do not come with the theme package. In some cases they may be installed using the dummy content file. When shopping for a theme, think of it as a photo album or scrapbook: you bring the contents.

Please note: "Premium" does not necessarily mean "high quality." In the world of WordPress themes it's a marketing term that simply means "not free." I have seen some amazing free themes, and have purchased some horrendous premium themes. Your due diligence, plus chapters 2 and 3, will help ensure you get the a quality theme that will fit your needs regardless of whether it is a "premium" theme or not.

Free Themes

These are free-to-download themes that you can use without restrictions. But, there are also "freemium" themes where you download a theme that has limited features and functionality of another "premium" theme. The difference here is very similar to free versus "lite" apps that you download to your smartphone. You should expect the lite version to be more like a trial version as they tend to have limited features.

Free

Free means that the developer is allowing you to download the theme without having to pay for it. You can find free-to-download themes in the WordPress Themes Directory, on developer/freelancer websites, and on some company/agency sites that develop themes (they occasionally give one away as loss leader to get you to try it.)

I know it seems a bit much to have to describe what a free theme is, but these really are quite different than the "fremium" themes you will come across (which I'll cover next.) Free themes are typically full-featured themes, and they range from drab and boring to absolutely stunning design.

The main reason developers give away full-featured themes is to get noticed, especially when they are just starting out. It's like a calling card or portfolio piece, and since they are free, word gets out and the downloads start to add up. Another reason to give them away for free is as a beta test: allowing people to download and use so developers can work out the bugs. Once the theme is stable, developers might decide a theme is good enough to be sold in a marketplace.

> **The Ozzie Theme.** I created a free theme called "Ozzie." It's a responsive theme showcasing featured images on posts and pages. Images and videos are also responsive down to small screens like iPhones. You can read more and download it here: http://ozzie.tristandenyer.com/

Freemium

These themes are just put out with the intent of you 'test driving' it. Meaning, the theme's functions are limited in scope, and eventually you will be asked or prompted to purchase the full version.

This trial or lite version is not to be confused with demos or previews of themes where you are directed to visit a live version of a theme that is running on a website — typically with dummy content—to show how it works. The freemium is meant to be installed and activated on your site in the hopes that you like it and want to buy the full-featured version.

This is not just a WordPress theme concept, and the "freemium" model of doing business is not a new one. In fact, you probably use a freemium app or program every day. Sites like LinkedIn, Facebook and Buffer let you use their app for free. If you want to get added features, better delivery rates, or be able to use it beyond a set period, you have to pay LinkedIn, Facebook and Buffer.

> **Searching for freemium themes.** The term "freemium" is used in a derogatory way to describe the practice of creating a lite version of a premium theme. It's not a positive marketing term like "premium" is, so no one really uses it to describe their theme. You may see terms like "lite," or "trial", but not freemium.
>
> Because of this, you may have issues doing a web search for "freemium" themes depending on the search engine you use. For example, when using the search phrase "freemium WordPress themes" Yahoo delivers results that actually use the term "freemium", whereas Google ignores what you typed and searches for *free premium WordPress themes*. Not the same thing. I recommend using quotes around your Google search to avoid this problem.

Boilerplate Themes

Boilerplate themes are also called starter or developer themes. Do not confuse "starter theme" with one that you should start with as a person new to WordPress. They mean starter in the same way a baker does: something that is already prepared (fermented, as in the case of sourdough) to get the development started a bit faster. If you have ever seen a hot rod rolling chassis, boilerplates are a lot like that: a lot of structural parts preassembled and waiting for all the custom, pretty parts to get added.

> **Not minimal.** Boilerplate is not the same as the term "minimal" that you will see bandied about when describing themes. In that sense, the design is minimal in that it is sparse with little to no visual elements (though it could be feature-minimal, too.)

Developers that use boilerplate themes benefit from the work of one or a dozen other developers who have produced a lightweight and tested option for theme development, as opposed to starting to build a theme from scratch. Some boilerplate themes like Skeleton, Bones, and Roots have gone through numerous revisions and are now really solid, economically viable starting points for developers doing custom themes. In some cases, theme developers have their own boilerplates they created over the years.

For those of you looking to design and develop your own theme, I highly recommend starting with one of the themes mentioned above. Documentation with boilerplate themes is typically extensive, produced with the intention of arming people with enough information to customize the theme's code, whereas inline developer documentation with premium themes can be sparse or missing.

> **No updates!** And here is where I contradict myself. Throughout this book I say "keep your theme up to date" over and over to the point of you getting sick of it. And for good reason (which we will get into later.) With boilerplate themes though, your developer typically modifies ("forks") the original theme files, so you cannot update the boilerplate theme as you would a free or premium theme.

Full-Custom Themes

It is important to differentiate "full-custom" themes from "customized" themes (also called "agency themes") which are premium or free themes redesigned and or recoded for a client.

Full-custom themes typically start with a boilerplate theme (see above), but some are created from scratch where the developer hand codes every line of the theme to suit your needs. This is not often the case because starting with a boilerplate theme is fairly common practice and saves the developer a lot of time.

In the case of custom themes, your features are, for the most part, only limited by your budget and the ability of the developer. This is different from premium themes where the features are already chosen for you.

What Makes Each Theme Unique?

I don't really want to compare themes to fingerprints or snowflakes, but each one really is individual and unique. Depending on who coded it, the purpose of it, and when they coded it, the theme could be very different from the previous one they built. In fact, 100 developers could code 100 themes based on the exact same Photoshop design file, and they would all be coded 100 unique ways.

With each WordPress Core update comes more changes, and theme developers need to stay up to date with all the new changes to the actions, filters, functions, APIs, loops, hooks and more. These changes, for better or worse, have an impact on how themes are developed.

Built on standards; unique by parameters

While I said all themes are unique, they are essentially built using a collection of standards set by WordPress.org. Consider each standard 1-5 lines of code, like this tag that displays the title of a Post or Page:

```
<title><?php wp_title(); ?></title>
```

Above is the bare minimum a developer needs to make it work, but many of these have parameters and other customizations to enhance them. Developers can express the above tag in different ways, such as:

```
<title><?php wp_title( '|', true, 'right' ); ?></title>
```

```
<title><?php wp_title('|'); ?></title>
```

Without going into details here, you can see that WordPress.org sets the standards for theme development, and it is up to the developer to expand on it to suit their needs or client's requests. Some of these can be used together to create a string of information, such as:

```
<title><?php wp_title('|'); ?><?php bloginfo('name'); ?></title>
```

Without knowing a single thing about PHP code, you can see that the outcome of your data depends on the way your theme was crafted. In the example above, search engines will see the title of the page followed by the name of your blog like this:

```
A great page about squirrels | Tristan Denyer's Awesome Website
```

These details matter

The reason I am going this deep into how a developer crafts a theme is that you will be judged on it every time Google and other search engines visit your site. How these search engines "see" the structure of your website is the heart of SEO. If it is haphazardly crafted without any thought to order and what search engines prefer/expect to see, your site's ranking will suffer because Google or Yahoo would have a hard time properly indexing your web pages.

Good theme developers know not only how to code the theme to deliver the right information, but how to display the pieces in a logical order for humans and search engines, and also know when enough information is enough.

The invisible design. There is a side of theme development that goes unseen, is rarely talked about, but makes up the bulk of *good* theme development. Most people experience the look and feel of the theme or the multitude of features made available in the Admin Panel. What is often unsaid or forgotten is the effort that went into all the choices that made that theme great.

Many themes sold in marketplaces today are designed and developed by one person. This person designs the user experience (UX), the user-interface (UI), the structure of the SEO opportunities, the information architecture (IA), the interaction design (IxD), and in some cases custom Theme Options screens in the Admin Panel, the demo/preview website, as well as the theme's marketing pages/website.

After all that, we haven't even talked about the actual coding of the theme yet, or the time they spend researching the theme market ecosystem for what customers want as well as what WordPress.org is working on for the next release. What you see above is often the only part of the theme you actually enjoy and experience. The 30 to 300-plus hours it takes to code, test and support a theme are minor in comparison to the hundreds of hours spent keeping up on that list of things that really make the theme interesting and modern.

During the process of designing the UX, UI, SEO, IA, IxD and so on, numerous choices have to be made about what code to use, as we talked about previously. Choose the wrong parameter or variable, and it can have a great effect on the UX, UI, SEO, IA, IxD, as well as how successful the theme will be in the marketplace.

Before You Start Looking for a Theme

If you are someone that likes to just "wing it" when it comes to new things, you might want reconsider that style while working with WordPress. The theme you choose can range from a goose that lays golden eggs to an albatross around your neck. Whether you are looking for your first theme, or your next one, this list can help you select the theme you need.

.COM For those of you on the WordPress.com platform, know that you are limited to themes found in the Admin Panel's Themes screen (Appearance > Themes). You may or may not be able to find all the things we go over below in a theme. And you can ignore anything about plugins since you cannot install them.

Planning Ahead

Let's think of this as planning to go on a hiking camp trip: you've got things you need (tent, sleeping bag, food), things you want (solar shower, s'mores, cushy sleeping pad), and things you might need incase of situations like rain, bears, poison ivy, etc.

The size of your pack and amount you can carry is like your website's budget, and what you can actually fit inside it is like the features of your website.

You get together the things you *need* first, and see how much room is left in your pack. You have some room for the cushy sleeping pad, so that goes in, until you realize there is a good chance for rain and you'll need a tarp and rain gear. The pack is getting heavy, and it will only make the hike in (and out) that much more miserable. Something has to go, but what?

Every time I have built a website for someone, I always feel like the leader in a hiking trip saying that some item (feature) won't fit or isn't possible because they have reached their carry limit. Again, in terms of a website that limit is the size of their 'pack' and could be determined by their budget—the time they have to manage the site, their server space, and myriad other things.

The following checklist is to help you think of what you *need* and *want* your website to do, as well as what you should have incase things go wonky (like a backup system.) The size and weight of your 'pack' is determined by you, your client and or the web developer you are working with.

Don't Lose Sight of Your Mission

Whether you are building an online store for a skate shop, or a simple blog to keep friends and family informed of your new baby, there is a mission or principle reason for doing it. Not knowing the mission or even losing sight of it during the theme-shopping process may result in selecting an albatross of a theme.

Skate shop example

Your mission statement should be succinct and tweetable: no more than 140 characters in length should be sufficient. To prove it's possible, we will use the example from the Cruz Skate Shop online storefront: "*As a skater-owned roller derby shop, we seek to provide skating gear, protective equipment, and information to all levels of roller skaters.*"

Taking the tweetable mission statement for Cruz, we can infer that we need a website that:

- Has space for an "About us" section/page to help establish the owners as being knowledgable, industry professionals.

- Has an online storefront to sell skating goods, including being able to showcase, describe and categorize items for purchase.

- Has a blog section for informative articles.

Three bullet points may not look like much, but using this short list while creating the checklist below will help ensure that major needs of the business and website don't fall by the wayside. That may seem unlikely, but I have seen it happen time and time again: a site owner—or even a whole team—forgetting to include a major piece of functionality.

In the next chapter I will talk about emailing a three-sentence summary to a developer.

Three bullet points above converted to three sentences in an email… boom! Done. Easy.

Family blog example

Think this doesn't apply to your family blog? I came up with this tweetable statement: *"A private family blog to keep relatives informed about the imminent birth of our second son, as well as our first son's recitals."*

Sounds like they will need:

- site-wide password protection to keep it private

- a blog for the periodic news updates on the pregnancy and children's activities

- something to share their first son's love of music: maybe video and audio galleries?

> **What's your tweetable mission statement?** You don't have to be on Twitter to do this. A 20-25 word statement should suffice. Keep in mind that a well-crafted statement also serves double-duty as a great piece in your overall SEO strategy in that it can help people find your site.

The Checklist

Below are a list of questions I ask clients and friends when we go through this process. Some of these questions can be answered as you read them, others may require you to do some research to get the answers. Overall, this will help you understand what you are looking for in a theme as well as keep you on track so you don't get stupefied by fancy spinning rims.

Mini-books could be created to expand on each of these questions. But, I'll spare you and simply follow them up with some highlights to consider. Ready?

What is the main motif, or subject of your website? Audio, video, blog, store, photography?

Knowing this will help you look for themes built for these services and features in mind. If you are building a photography website and you start looking in the "nonprofit themes" section of a marketplace, you might have a hard time finding a theme.

> **Pro Tip:** WordPress 3.6+ has built in audio, video and image gallery capabilities. You may not need your theme to do this for you (or, as I like to say: You may not need your theme ignoring and overriding these awesome, native features.)

Do you need a blog?

Some themes do not have a blog section styled or even thought out. Odd, I know, but some owners don't need a blog, and it saves development time. You may not need a blog now, but know that you don't save any money by getting a theme without blog support (unless you are getting a fully custom built theme, then you may actually save money by not having the developer even bother with it.)

If yes (to having a blog), do you need recent Posts to show on the home page? In the side bar of interior pages? Anywhere else?

Having your blog roll be the home page is native to WordPress. But, incorporating recent blog posts into a styled homepage is up to the developer to code into the "home.php" theme file. Know that placing recent posts in the sidebar is a feature of the native WordPress Recent Posts widget. Having them show in the main content area of a Page is up to the theme developer, or could be done with a plugin.

Do you need to be able to feature certain Pages on your homepage?

Placing featured Pages on the homepage is possible, but up to the developer to code into the "home.php" theme file (or by using a plugin.) Placing them in the sidebar is a feature of the native WordPress Pages widget (though it's a bit lacking in customization options.) Having featured Pages show in the main content area of a Page or Post is up to the theme developer to implement, or could be done with a plugin.

Do you need a slider on the homepage? On interior pages? On blog posts?

(AKA carousels, slideshow, rotators, slide decks, …) While sliders seem standard-issue nowadays, not all themes have them. And not all themes have the ability to show unique sliders on other pages. There are a *bazillion* plugins out there that can place a *gazillion* differently styled sliders anywhere on your website.

Pro Tip #1: Sliders are a proven waste of your time and resources. Don't use them. *Whoa! What?!* I know, right? How can something that is on almost every website be a bad thing? Because visitors don't stick around for the 2ⁿᵈ, or 3ʳᵈ slide, they generally ignore them.

A study of the University of Notre Dame (http://weedygarden.net/2013/01/carousel-stats/) and Siemens (http://www.nngroup.com/articles/auto-forwarding/) websites made it pretty clear that sliders, carousels, accordions and rotators may be pretty to look at, but are ineffective to helping your visitors. Even Brad Frost, a thought leader in our industry, weighed in on it (http://bradfrostweb.com/blog/post/carousels/), which can be summed up with "most carousels simply don't need to exist."

So, listen to the data and drop the slider. Just use one image/slide at a time will do.

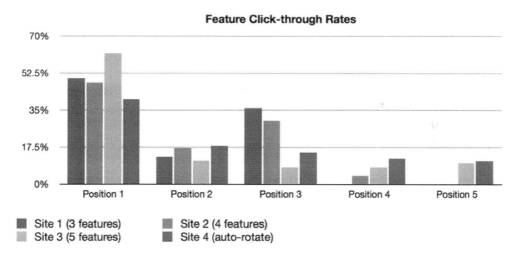

Image showing click-through rates for sliders on 4 websites. Each were set to auto-play (or auto-forward after a set period of time.) © Copyright Jan 2013, WeedyGarden.net/, source http://weedygarden.net/2013/01/carousel-stats/

> **Pro Tip #2:** If you rely heavily on sliders and revolving images, I highly recommend using a well-supported, paid plugin and not the native slideshow feature of the theme you chose (if possible.) Many sliders have numerous fancy options, and with those options comes a lot of code. Much of this code relies on browser capabilities and advanced coding practices that require a lot of maintenance on the part of the developer.
>
> A slider that is maintained as part of a theme is essentially just one of many parts of that theme. In order to fix any bugs or issues with the slider, they would have to push out a theme update. Not all themes are set to receive update notifications in the Admin Panel (or even alert you via email), so you may not be notified of the fix.
>
> Purchasing a well-supported slider such as the Soliloquy plugin (http:// soliloquywp.com/) that has "automatic plugin updates" can ensure that the sliders work well into the future. Best of all, all your work that went into setting up the sliders won't be lost when you switch themes (see chapter 12 about switching themes.)

Does the slider need to auto*magic*ally feature the latest post and link to it? Or sticky posts? Or featured images in posts? Or have the ability to show videos?

(Yes, auto*magic*ally, because let's get real, some of this stuff on the surface looks and works like magic.) So many options are available in slideshows these days. If you are so bold as to listen to the data above and choose not to use a slider, then your job is done here and cheers to you! If not, review the sliders and be sure to check them out on the theme's demo page. If you can get your hands on the theme documentation before purchasing, look to see how tedious it is to maintain the contents for the slider. Some can be a nightmare, while others are, well, *automagical.*

Does the new theme support widgets?

While the vast majority of themes do support widgets, some minimal and boilerplate themes may not. I have no idea why a developer would choose to not widgetize (create areas for widgets) at least the sidebar in a theme, but it happens. Many plugins rely on being used as a widget to allow you to place it in your sidebar(s) and other widgetized areas, so make sure your theme supports widgets, or is "widgetized."

Do you need the website to be responsive?

To understand exactly what responsive web design is can fill a whole book. In short, it's a technique that allows your website to resize to fit smartphones, tablets and larger desktop screens. It's so your users don't have to zoom in on their phones to read it. Still confused? Don't worry, it's can take a bit to wrap your head around this concept of your website's elements actually resizing and shifting around to better fit small screens.

Do a web search on "what is responsive web design" for the latest info on how we are approaching this technique. But, know that not all websites need to be responsive. Do a web search for "do I need a responsive website" for tips on whether you need it. Some themes even allow your admin and or visitors to turn off/on responsiveness.

What browsers does your theme need to support?

The short of it is that every browser and every version of that browser renders websites in a unique way. It can be as subtle as the text readability, or as serious as not being able to recognize certain page elements or styles at all. Clicking on any one of the numerous features at http://caniuse.com/ will show you just how differently browsers and their versions can render any given website.

If Google Analytics is installed on your current site, you can use it to see the most popular browser your visitors use. You want to make sure your theme supports the browsers your visitors are using, or else things on your site can look wonky or not work for them. You really only need to look at the latest 3-6 months of data to get a good read on what browsers people are using.

The important thing you are looking for is Internet Explorer (IE) users. IE is a *huge* pain-point for web developers because versions 6, 7, 8, and 9 lag behind what other browsers like Firefox, Safari and Chrome could do. If 30% of your visitors are still using IE 8, then you need to make sure your theme is tested and supports IE 8. Keep in mind many developers are no longer supporting IE 6 and 7, with many starting to drop support for IE 8 and 9 too.

The main reason these browsers are being dropped is HTML5—the markup language many themes are built on today—is not supported by IE 9 and below. In order to do so requires a bunch of JavaScript to help it conform to the new features offered by HTML5.

> **Pro Tip:** Comparing the last 3 months to data from 6 months or a year ago can show you trends. Let's say all versions of Internet Explorer (IE) browsers made up 33% of your visitors last year at this time, then 6 months ago it fell to 27%, and today it's 19%. That shows a trend toward fewer IE users over time. You can estimate that in the next 6 months IE users could fall below 15% for your website, making it less important than other browsers.
>
> Also keep in mind that Firefox was once a very popular browser. Trending showed it on a path to overtaking all other browsers. Then came Google's Chrome, and it has become the darling of the industry today. If you bought a theme in 2009, Google's Chrome was barely on the radar. Today it's the most used browser in many countries.
>
> Bug fixes and cross-browser support is just another reason you want to be sure your theme is actively maintained with periodic updates.

Do you need your website to support translation for international users?

Some themes come with this support built in. Depending on the native language you intend to write your website copy in, you may need to offer the visitor a way to have it translated for them to their native language. Keep in mind that while translation is improving each year, this is never perfect, and can provide some interesting outcomes. If your site is very technical, you may want to consider a paid service that deals with the extended vocabulary pertinent to your website.

Many themes also have a file called rtl.css to help support languages that read from right-to-left (RTL) such as Arabic or Hebrew text. But, it's not just text that is affected. Images you align to the left need to flip to the right. Same goes for comments, Twitter feed, the content of widgets and so on. Some may need the sidebar to flip to the other side of the page.

Does your website need to be accessible and Section 508 Standards Compliant?

I hate to say it, but this is where theme developers fall short. It is pretty rare that I have seen a truly 508 compliant theme (which is required by all U.S. government agencies, some educational institutions and any site that is for low- or no-vision visitors.)

Coding a website or theme to be accessible and 508 compliant requires certain tags, attributes and other code to be present in specific places, and in a specific hierarchical order—much like an outline for a research paper. This architecture is intended to help the user navigate, as well as describe the contents of the website to them, like forms and navigation menus, for example.

The knock-on effect to having an accessible website is that it makes for great SEO. Accessibility helps web search engines (like Google) understand your website better since they now don't have to guess what an element's intended purpose is. While viewing a website, you can right-click on the screen and select "view source" to get a glimpse of what a Google web crawler sees.

Do you need your Pages and Posts to have social sharing buttons?

You've likely seen these on a *bazillion* web pages: little buttons or icons prompting you to share the page on Twitter, Facebook, Pinterest and more. Some themes come with these built into its functionality, while others rely on plugins to add them.

> **Pro Tip:** Drop the social sharing buttons. Like sliders, these are proving to be ineffective in getting people to share your Pages and Posts. The reason is that the vast majority of people understand how to share a web page without using the social sharing buttons on the page.
>
> The major problem with having these buttons on your site is that they slow down the loading of the page. The reason for this is that each button (be it 3, 5 or a dozen) has to reach out to their respective server and retrieve a separate JavaScript file in order to make them work. If you are displaying a number of "shares", it has to retrieve that information too. All of this takes time.
>
> This can cause other elements and content on your page to not load while it is busy loading all the files it takes to run the social media buttons. I've seen these social sharing buttons slow a site down by as much as 10 seconds, which may cost you users, as people tend to leave a slow loading page. More info on that here: http://www.nytimes.com/2012/03/01/technology/impatient-web-users-flee-slow-loading-sites.html

Is someone asking for SEO?

You'll see this in theme marketing pages as "SEO ready", "SEO Optimized", "SEO built in" and so on. But, honestly, if a theme touts it's SEO readiness, it's probably bullshit.

"SEO" is vying for most overused marketing buzzword in our industry.

> **Choose SEO you can take with you.** A big drawback to using the SEO features in a theme is that when you switch themes, it's gone. Any SEO title or description customizations you made stay with the old theme; you have to type it all in again on the new theme. Just use the "Yoast's WordPress SEO plugin." It's the best SEO plugin out there, does more than any theme's SEO can, and you'll take any and all SEO customizations with you to your next theme.

Are you needing each section of your site to have custom/unique sidebars?

Look for the term "custom sidebars" or "unlimited sidebars" or both. Don't worry if it doesn't, there's a bunch of great free and premium plugins for managing custom sidebars.

What are you planning on placing in the sidebars? Latest Vimeo videos? Twitter feed? MailChimp email sign up? Affiliate banners?

Some themes have this functionality built in, but there are tons of plugins to help get certain objects and feeds into a sidebar. It's good to know what you plan on placing in there to know what to look for. Things like email sign up are rare in themes, but as you guessed it, there's a plugin (or 12) for that.

> **The API call.** Keep in mind that many features that reach out to a third-party like MailChimp or Twitter rely on APIs to connect them (for now, just think of an API as your website having a secret phone number for your Twitter feed that it can call when needed.) These APIs can and do change over time to become more secure or use the latest technologies.
>
> See the API entry in the Glossary section in the back of this book for the short story on the recent Twitter API issue.

Do you have a specific font in mind for your headers? Or at least want a selection of fonts to choose from?

Like sliders, this is almost standard on most themes, but not all. Today, many of the premium themes I see are using Google Fonts, which are quite extensive so you shouldn't have a problem finding a nice font to work with.

But, as with many fun things on the web, not all browsers display these embedded web fonts very well. In some cases like Internet Explorer or other browsers on a PC, the fonts can actually look quite pixelated and ugly. Browsers on Macs make fonts look smooth, closer to printed text, even on non-Retina screens. Be sure to view the theme demo site on a PC and a Mac, if possible—the difference in readability can be startling to some.

Cufon fonts. Cufon is a JavaScript file that embeds fonts using the HTML canvas element. I know, a bit techie, but this feature helps produce smoother lettering, as well as fix some size and rendering issues. This is a popular option for theme developers, but I take great pains in seeing it used since it wraps each word in a ton of code. See example below of what it takes for the website to tell the browser how to simply render the word "information":

```
<cufon class="cufon cufon-canvas" alt="information "
style="width: 114px; height: 24px;"><canvas width="132"
height="25" style="width: 132px; height: 25px; top: 0px;
left: -1px;"></canvas><cufontext>information </cufontext></
cufon>
```

The JavaScript does all the work of wrapping the word for you, but the problem is two-fold: one word of text turns into about 30 words of code. 50 words turn into about 1500 words of code. This makes the website render slower in the browser. The second problem I have with it is that when a user tries to highlight the text it makes it difficult to do so and does it in chunks, often missing the first word.

If you use Cufon, be sure to only use it for headers and not on paragraph text. This will greatly reduce the amount of code needed to render the text on the page. Again, do the math.

With Google fonts or other methods using a CSS rule called @font-face, that same word is rendered without wrapping it in a bunch of code, though it does not always render perfectly in all browsers. Lately, my preference when building a website is to design the site so it shows Internet Explorer users something they are used to, like Verdana (which does render nicely), and everyone else the embedded or Google font.

Do you need to be able to upload your logo? Is it horizontal, vertical or square?

Depending on the real estate the theme designer gave you for the logo, you might be trying to put a rectangle logo into a square hole. If your logo is much taller than it is wide, good luck! Most themes seem to be designed for thin, horizontal logos.

Are you planning on selling items on your website? How many? 1... 12... 3,000? And are they physical items (requiring shipping) or digital downloads, or both?

There are so many things to consider when choosing and setting up a store on your WordPress website that it could fill another 200-page book. Some themes come with a storefront built in (usually an embedded plugin—see chapter 9), whereas others rely on you adding a storefront plugin.

> **STOP!** If you are considering an online storefront, I highly recommend you do NOT use a storefront or cart built into a theme. I highly recommend you use a professional grade, paid plugin such as ecommerce plugins from Pippin's Pluggins (http://pippinsplugins.com/), WooCommerce (http://www.woothemes.com/woocommerce/), and Jigoshop (http://jigoshop.com/), to name a few.

> By setting up your store using a plugin, you will be able to swap out your theme without losing your store inventory, customer records, gift certificates, payment gateway, and a lot more. If you have never set up an online store before, know that it is something you only want to do once. Seriously. Do not lock up all that information in a theme.

> Also, keep in mind that you are dealing with money, taxes, people's personal information, and in some States/Countries, you may have very strict laws governing your online sales. You don't want to go about this haphazardly. Work with a developer that specializes in ecommerce.

Ecommerce Pro Tip: If you are selling 1-10 items, you may want to consider using a service such as Gumroad. You can still have a website with Pages listing your items for sale, but the "buy now" button/link points to your Gumroad page where customers can purchase the item.

This can help alleviate having to set up and manage a storefront for only a few items. It can also place all the worrisome security and compliance issues on a third party like Gumroad, and not on you or your team.

Do you need a gallery for photos, images, videos, or Instagram?

Today, numerous themes have gallery options. What you need to look for is how it is handled in the Admin Panel. Is it complicated to set up? Does it automatically pull images in? Are there plugins that can handle it better?

If you intend to set up numerous galleries, keep in mind that a plugin is a much better option since you will be able to switch themes without having to start over from scratch.

Do you need a forum added to your site? Or is your whole site specifically a forum?

Some themes come with this, though it is not common. If your entire site is a forum, I would recommend looking for a theme that is designed primarily to be a forum. Same goes for forums as it does for online storefronts: both can swell to be a great amount of information. Consider a forum plugin so that you can swap out the theme later, and even be able to separate the two later.

Do you need a secure area (not the same as the Admin Panel) that users/clients can log into?

These are typically useful for having special pages for clients or subscribers. You can use the native WordPress "Private" Post/Page, but I recommend looking into a theme or plugin that can handle a secure area without having to give the user access to the Admin Panel.

Do you need a 'Contact Us' form? If so, what fields do you need? Do users need to be able to upload files via this form?

While most themes come with basic form submission of name, email, subject, message, look for additional features like file upload, or the ability to customize a larger form with additional fields and field types. A huge plus is a form that can accept file uploads and store them on a Dropbox, Google Drive or RackSpace account—basically, offsite. I never liked the idea of people uploading their files to the same place where my website lives.

Don't Paint Yourself Into a Corner

Some of you may see a recurring theme in my list above: keep features as plugins so you can take them with you, and not locked up in a theme.

Feature debt

You will inevitably see a mountain of themes that can do everything you have on your list, and then some. They'll tout things like "No plugins needed!", "Plugin-free", and "Zero plugin theme". While this sounds easy and so thoughtful of the developer, this requires you taking on feature debt.

Feature debt (or design debt) in WordPress themes is the act of taking the quick and easy push-button-choice of an all-inclusive theme, where later down the road you will have to pay a much bigger price if you ever need to switch themes. That "price" is the time and money necessary to build a new site when all your settings, store inventory, and/or galleries are locked up in the old theme.

You can think of feature debt as a too-good-to-be-true home loan that required no down payment, and no payments for the first 6 months. If you are thinking that some all-inclusive theme is going to save you a weekend's worth of work, I can guarantee you that when it comes time to switch the theme you will spend weeks just trying to copy over all the information and settings that you have set up over the life of the previous theme. Any features controlled by a plugin will remain in place and—in the vast majority of cases—work with the new theme.

Frogs first; ice cream later

Successful company executives and productivity experts swear that tackling the biggest and ugliest problem first thing in the morning is key to having a productive day. It is applied to projects, as well. You may have heard this Mark Twain quote in relation to that idea:

> "Eat a live frog first thing in the morning and nothing worse will happen to you the rest of the day." — Mark Twain

I know that the preparations such as the list above, the mission statement, and having to research some plugins may be tedious, and frankly, may not be as much fun as shopping for themes. But, it's your live frog. Eat it first thing and the rest of your theme shopping will be a breeze, and turn out better for it.

Myth busting: plugins are okay

For years, there has been a mantra going around that "plugins are bad", or that they slow your website down. This is not entirely true. The truth is that badly coded plugins may slow your website down and or overtax your server, while well-crafted plugins don't.

In recent years we have seen a surge in owners placing numerous widgets and plugins on websites that require third-party interactions. Services like Twitter, Facebook, Instagram, countless social sharing buttons, GitHub status feeds, Flickr galleries, advertising partners and more. Each one of these has to make a call out to a third-party server and wait for a response in order to retrieve the data to display on the website. The more of these types of plugins you have installed on your site the slower it is going to load.

> **Further reading.** I highly suggest taking a moment to read the article "Functionality: Plugins vs Themes" written by developer Pippin Williamson: http://wp.tutsplus.com/articles/general/functionality-plugins-vs-themes/

Getting the Right Theme for You

In chapter 1C, I described the four types of themes (purchased, free, boilerplate, and full-custom.) In this chapter I will cover how to find the right theme for you based on these theme types.

This is by far the hardest concept to convey to people. Like buying a house, there is no single, straightforward way to do it that covers all the buying decisions you will face. Since listing every possible way is near impossible, we'll be covering an entry-level approach to finding a theme that should cover the vast majority of users (even if you don't consider yourself "entry-level.")

Before you begin with this chapter, make sure you understand how Parent and Child themes work (chapter 1A.) Not all themes are structured this way, but if you choose to use this method some of the caveats below in regards to swapping out themes may not apply.

.COM For those of you on the WordPress.com platform, know that you are limited to themes found in the WordPress Theme Directory. Go to the Themes screen in your Admin Panel under Appearance > Themes. (As of 3.8) you will see sections for "Trending," "Popular," "Newest," "All," "Free," and "Premium." Boilerplate themes, externally developed custom themes and plugins do not apply to you; they are only available to self-hosted website users.

Before You Start: Plugins

Before you jump into finding a theme that fits your list of requirements, know that you may need to supplement your theme with some plugins. Not all themes will be able to do everything on your list.

In the case where you find a great theme that is missing a feature (or three) from your list, a plugin (or three) can add that functionality to your theme.

Plugins are outside the scope of this book, but can be important to some themes. So, I have to point you in the right direction for now and cover them in an upcoming book. Until then, you can follow these steps to finding a plugin to add functionality to your theme:

1) Visit your Admin Panel's Plugin screen (Plugins > Add New > Search) or http://wordpress.org/plugins/ and use the search box to find the functionality you need. For example: If I want to add SEO controls to my site, I do a search for "SEO" (without quotes.)

2) In the Admin Panel's list of results, click on the "Details" link under the name (or click the name) to view the plugin details to do some basic research on the plugin. You are looking to see if it does what you need it to do.

3) While in this detail page, review the ratings. Does it have enough ratings with a certain level stars to make you feel okay in using it? (I tend to be a 4-star and up kind of person, but know that sometimes a great plugin gets 3 stars.)

4) Now check out the tabs along the top for more details about the plugin. Pay special attention to the "Installation" tab to make sure you know how to install it (some have special installation steps.)

5) If you like what you see, click "Install Now." Then activate the plugin. PRO TIP: Always back up your site before you activate plugins. See chapter 5.

6) You should check your site to make sure the functionality you desired is working. Know that some plugins require you to do additional steps to get the plugin working on your site.

If you don't find a plugin via the Admin Panel search method above, you will likely need to do some web searches to find WordPress plugins outside the WordPress Plugin Directory that fit your needs. The key here is to include the words "WordPress plugin" along with the functionality you are looking to add. For example: If I want to add SEO controls to my site, I do a Google search for "WordPress plugin SEO" (without quotes.)

The steps for researching plugins via a web search can be varied and beyond the scope of this book. Though, you could start by using the same due diligence as I've listed out previously in this section, and then take steps similar to what you would do when researching premium themes (see below.)

A Purchased Theme

Where to purchase a theme

Purchased themes (or "premium" themes) are often sold via the developer's website or in online marketplaces. Let's first go over the main differences:

A developer's website selling themes:

- Is typically owned and managed by a freelance developer or company of developers and designers

- Will showcase a small- to medium-sized collection of themes they developed

- Will support only the themes they designed and developed. Though, some may be for hire to help design and develop a custom theme.

- Examples are WooThemes, Elegant Themes, Rodrigo Galindez (http://www.rodrigogalindez.com/themes/modernist/).

An online marketplace selling themes:

- Can be owned/managed by non-developers and developers (much like a boutique selling dresses can be owned/managed by people who don't know how to sew, but have a conversational grasp of its construction and materials.)

- Typically relies on freelance developers and companies to upload themes to sell.

- Will showcase a medium-sized to massive collection of themes.

- Will support only the themes they designed and developed. Though, some may be for hire to help design and develop a custom theme (but work for hire will need to take place outside the marketplace.)

- Examples are ThemeForest and Mojo Themes.

> **For self-hosted WordPress installations**, you typically buy the theme via a marketplace, download it immediately and install it on your site (see chapter 6 for installing a theme.)
>
> **For WordPress.com users**, you cannot upload themes, so you are limited to themes found in the WordPress theme marketplace via the Themes screen in your Admin Panel under Appearance > Themes > Premium link.

Prepare yourself

Just going to let you know up front that researching premium themes takes time. Definitely more than 10 minutes. A more realistic timeframe is about two hours, possibly more depending on any particular requirements you/your client has for a site.

What? Two hours or more?! Know that there are dozens of websites selling themes, each with dozens—sometimes hundreds—of themes for sale. Some have you sort through the collection by only seeing thumbnail images of the theme; others only show you great lists of features without the thumbnail image. You are going to have to click through most of these to see the theme in action.

Every theme is different, so you will be spending a lot of time taking their themes for a 'test drive' by viewing their preview websites. During this time you will likely get lost in all the cool features you never knew existed. That can cause the list we made in chapter 2 to change (which is okay, to an extent.) And that can cause you to have to visit themes again to see if they now fit your new list.

Give yourself a good solid window of a couple hours for looking through themes. Ten minutes here and there will not suffice as proceeding in that fashion is more likely to land you with a real dud of a theme.

How to shop for premium themes

Shopping for premium themes is like shopping for shoes. Many of you have bought a pair of great looking shoes only to find out they hurt your feet. You likely knew better while trying them on in the shop, but thought they would break in. Your feet don't always win, and when it comes to themes there is no break-in period, it either works or it doesn't. (One exception is if you plan on customizing the theme with a Child Theme, we will get into that in chapter 11.)

I wish all theme marketplaces worked like Amazon.com with filtering capabilities that allow me to select/deselect features and styles until I am left with a short list to go through. Unfortunately that is rarely the case, making the search harder.

To help guide you through the assorted marketplaces, the following list outlines how I shop for themes on most sites. (Grab your laptop/desktop and a tablet or smartphone if you have one, since you will want to see what any given theme looks like across these devices.)

1) Start by understanding that almost every theme out there can make a decent to great website, but not every theme is right for you. Knowing that, you are shopping by eliminating themes that don't work for you. Be critical and look for reasons a theme is NOT a good fit for your feature requirements, brand, and visitors.

2) Now, figure out which device matters most to you (Desktop? Mobile? Tablet?) If your website has to look amazing on a smartphone—or better yet, you know that is how most of your customers will be viewing it—then have it nearby so you can send preview/demo links to it and see how it responds to the smaller screen. PRO TIP: using the Ghostlab App or Adobe Edge Inspect App can greatly speed up this comparison process of viewing themes on numerous devices at once.

3) Start with reputable websites and marketplaces that specialize in WordPress themes. If a theme marketplace looks cheap and slapped together, leave and go to another—their support and quality is likely cheap and slapped together, or worse, it could be a consumer honeypot set up to get you to download compromised themes (more on this below.)

4) If the website has a search box (like ThemeForest,) try typing in your most important feature, such as "Twitter feed" or "video gallery." If there is no search box, go to step 5.

5) If available, look for a submenu where you can narrow the list down to a category. These categories could be titled "eCommerce", "Magazine", "Portfolio", "Business" and more. These are typically categorized by their design style, but some are based on specific theme features, such as having a store and checkout in "eCommerce."

6) At this point, you should be presented with a manageable list of themes. If you are on a website such as Elegant Themes that lists them as thumbnails, or on

one such as Theme Forest that lists details instead of an actual thumbnail, get ready to open dozens of pages.

7) From the list of theme thumbnails, select one that looks like it may satisfy your design style. Or, from the list of theme details, select one that looks like it may satisfy your feature list. You should now be on what is known as a "detail page" for the theme. Refrain from clicking on the "Preview" or "Demo" button: this will only waste time right now. On the detail page, read the details about each theme and compare that to your list in chapter 2. At this stage you will likely be ruling out themes very quickly because they don't fit your mandatory feature requirements (example: you found the theme is not responsive for mobile devices, or it is only a forum, or it's a single-page theme, & etc..)

8) When you find a detail page with features that fit your requirements, look for the "Preview" or "Demo" button so you can view the theme in action.

9) Now that the theme is in front of you, do your best to stay on task: you are looking for where this theme falls short or is problematic. Don't get too caught up in all the cool features and spinning rims. Themes designers and developers know what sells, and they will fill these demos with the shiniest of things to lure you in to buying it. Stay critical, and keep to your list so you come home with a theme that fits your needs.

10) Eventually you should have about 3-7 solid themes picked out. Be sure to save the URLs for their detail pages so you can visit them later. Even though one of these may be the one you purchase, it is a good idea to save links to the others that almost made it in the event that the one you bought doesn't work out.

> **Preview Tips:** Previews/demos are not always the same across all marketplaces. When shopping on the WordPress Themes Directory you will notice that the theme only shows 2-3 pages, and they usually look pretty stark in terms of content (probably to save space on WordPress' servers. They have over 2,600 themes!) When viewing themes on marketplaces such as ThemeForest you can expect to see robust demo websites with numerous pages containing a lot of content. After all, their themes are stored on the developer's server, and their intent is to get you to buy it.

How to choose one from the list

You now have a handful of themes to choose from. Buying all of them is not always an option, plus you certainly don't want to install all of them (we'll cover why in the following chapters.) It's time to whittle it down to one or two themes to purchase. In short, you are looking for the theme that closely fits your list of requirements, looks good, and works well.

As we mentioned above, you may find a theme that looks great, works well, but falls a little short on the features. It's time to do some research to see if there are plugins that can add that functionality back in. I recommend you search for plugins using the steps provided at the beginning of this chapter.

A theme that looks good and works well is a bit subjective. I tend to like minimal designs so pages load very fast, but that is really up to you. Put yourself in the shoes of your visitors and really take a step back to try and imagine what they will think of the design and the way it works. Ask a friend or colleague to view the preview/demo to give you feedback.

My recommendation is to not spend too much time trying to meet every feature requirement on your list. Many of them can be solved using a plugin. In fact, as I've said before, having a feature like a Twitter feed or online store that's powered by a plugin is a much smarter move than having the theme do it.

Pros of "premium" themes:

- **Options and customization:** The biggest draw to these types of themes are the myriad options and controls the developer builds into the theme, which for some users makes it very easy to customize without having to know any code. As features (such as slideshows and Twitter feeds) and options (such as background images and Google Fonts) become more popular, developers add them to the themes to make them more attractive to buyers. In the vast majority of cases, customizing a theme is done through the theme's options tab in your site's Admin Panel. In rare cases, you may be asked to select the theme customizations before you purchase/download it.

- **You own it:** once the purchase is complete and the theme is downloaded, you can install it on your site. You are not under contract to the seller, meaning you can do whatever you want with that theme. And they cannot take it back, or repossess it. In fact, the way WordPress is licensed, this goes for all themes. Do a web search for "WordPress themes GPL license" (no quotes) for more information on this hotly debated topic.

- **Support / forums:** Premium themes often come with direct support from the developer, or a community forum where other members may be able to answer your questions. Sometimes both. Most support I have seen comes in the form of email, forums or instant messaging (IM.) Do not expect 24-hour customer support via a phone number.

- **New features:** To me, this is a pro and a con. The pro side is that if you have a particularly eager and responsive developer behind the theme you bought, you could end up seeing new and exciting features being added to your theme's updates. Things like an Instagram or Vimeo gallery, or even extending the functionality to existing features to be used as widgets in sidebars where they once couldn't go. For the con side, see "Feature Bloat" below.

Features and options vs plugins. When starting out in WordPress it can be a bit tricky to wrap your head around the difference between a theme feature/option and a plugin. And more importantly, what this means to your database and your ability to swap out your theme with another. I cover this in detail in chapter 9.

Caution: In some cases where you make a request for support, I have seen developers ask for access to your site so they can inspect it and fix the problem. This is normal for some problems, which is why you should only deal with reputable marketplaces. Never give them your log in info, but instead make a new user with admin access. You can remove this user later.

Always completely backup your site and store the backup files in a safe place before you give another person access.

Cons of "premium" themes:

- **The everything omelet:** (slightly different than 'feature bloat' below) Some developers have a belief that the theme's sales will skyrocket if it can do everything (and that may be true.) So, s/he puts in every conceivable option and feature they know of into the theme. You may see 2-4 different ways to embed fonts (Google, Cufon, CSS), each with long lists of fonts to choose from. Some come with "50+ custom background" image choices and half a dozen icon styles in 12 colors, and over a dozen social media badges... you get my point. Be wary of themes that come with a million choices for everything. All of that comes with a lot of code to control it and render it, meaning your theme may require much more maintenance and attention from the developer. Which if you decided to go that route, would be another reason choose a theme developer that offers amazing support and continually updates their themes.

- **The exploits are well known, and easy to find:** There are a few things about these marketplace themes that make it a lot easier for people to hack WordPress sites. One is that some popular themes are sold to tens of thousands of people. Once an exploit (a weakness or backdoor in the code) is found in a theme—like the infamous timthumb.php exploit—it can be easily found on everyone else's site that has the same theme installed. It doesn't have to be activated, just installed (see Chapter 5 for the technical difference in the two terms "activated" and "installed.")

- **Update notifications don't always work:** While WordPress.com users can enjoy the fact that all of their themes have update notifications, know that not all self-hosted themes have the ability to alert you to an update. Some developers of themes for self-hosted sites will employ code that checks the version of the theme and notifies the admin of an update via the Admin Panel (the same way plugins and default WordPress themes do.) Think about the exploit problem above, and couple that with the fact that your theme may have an update available but has not alerted you. The developer may have found and fixed the exploit, but how are you going to know without checking their site every day or signing up for their email newsletter? To counter this problem, before purchasing ask the developer if their theme checks for the latest version (this version check typically does not apply to Boilerplate and Full-custom themes since they are built as one-off creations.)

- **Feature bloat:** The knock-on effect to new features being added to themes over time is that every new addition is more code your site has to load (as well as cache and backup, if you are doing so.) Depending on the feature added, and how it was implemented by the developer, this new code could be requested to load each time a page loads, even if you are not using the new feature anywhere on your site. The other side of this is that once they are coded into the theme some features may not be removed by the developer, even if that feature is now defunct.

- **"Free updates":** Some developers offer customers "free updates" for their themes, but these can often be limited to what are known as "dot upgrades"— an update from theme version 3.3 to 3.4, for example. In some cases, a developer/company may not support free updates for major releases, such as 3.9 to 4.0.

- **Limited support:** the real shocker comes when you find out the theme has spotty or limited support. This is more common when you buy themes from large marketplaces since they are typically developed and uploaded by a freelancer (or single developer.) I'm not knocking freelancers in any way, but instead stating the very real fact that this person is likely developing themes as a side project to their full-time job. They are also human, so taking vacations and getting sick are a reality. If the theme/marketplace does not come with a forum where other customers can collaborate on problems, you are relying on one person to answer your questions and fix bugs in the theme. Do some serious research on support for your theme *before* you buy it.

Pricing and support models are shifting fast. While I believe the pricing in the premium theme market has always been absurdly low—and more of a race to the bottom type pricing model—the prices have been steadily going up as of late. The reason for this is that marketplaces and developers have relied on selling the themes at scale (at the thousands) for a reasonable price (about $30-50 each.)

Recently, marketplaces and developers have found this to be unsustainable when coupled with free support for those thousands of customers. Expect prices to rise to around $55-100 on average, or for more marketplaces to decouple support and go to a paid model for that.

The last word on purchasing a theme

Keep in mind that the developer wants you to buy the theme. And like any overeager salesperson or marketer they sometimes are—oh, how can we say this—a little loose with the details. I have seen the word "dozens" used to describe "20" items. Terms like "infinite", "future-proof" and "bulletproof" get used a lot in this industry to make you feel good. Nothing in web design is "infinite", "future-proof" or "bulletproof." Look beyond the bullet points and start digging deep to see if it matches up to the list you made in chapter 2.

Know that each theme is in direct or near-direct competition with every other theme in that marketplace, and especially the free ones out there. As I said above, some developers will throw in every bell and whistle they know hoping it does everything on your list. That means there will likely be a few (or numerous) other options and features that you do not need, now or ever. This code is dead weight, and may cause potential conflicts with plugins you add down the road.

Look in the documentation for mentions of custom widgets that come with the theme.

If you start using these widgets, know that whatever content you place in them is tied to the theme. Meaning, if you decide to start using a different theme, it will not migrate any of those custom widgets over—the widget code is part of the old theme.

Same problem exists for Custom Fields being used to display certain pieces of metadata on a Page or Post. As in the custom widgets case, this is coded in the theme files and will not migrate over to a new theme, even if your new theme comes with Custom Fields.

A Free Theme

Free themes are available in numerous places, from the WordPress Themes Directory, some marketplaces, GitHub, developer sites and more. Some major theme marketplaces periodically give away a premium theme.

Where to find a good, free theme

Check out the WordPress Themes Directory first (http://wordpress.org/themes/.) You can also get there via the Admin Panel: Appearance > Themes > Add Themes button. While the Directory is not the flashiest marketplace out there, it does have over 2,600 clean, well-built themes to choose from.

These are not made to impress buyers with every bell and whistle known to man, but instead are solid, clean themes. They often rely on you finding the right plugin to add functionality, like a Twitter feed (which I feel is the way themes should be built.) I also like the fact that they are "subject to review" by the WordPress Themes team, as well as the WordPress community, meaning infected, compromised and broken themes get rooted out.

Feel like that they aren't worth your time? Think again. Check out the following free themes:

- **Spun**, by Caroline Moore, has over 317,000 downloads: http://wordpress.org/themes/spun

- **Irex Lite**, by Tikendra Maitry, has "custom follow us and contact widget" and layout options: http://wordpress.org/themes/irex-lite

- **Responsive**, by CyberChimps boasts "Theme features 9 Page Templates, 11 Widget Areas, 6 Template Layouts, 4 Menu Positions and more." Whoa: http://

wordpress.org/themes/responsive

Reputable sites are great places to not only get info on WordPress but also get tips on where to find themes. Check out sites such as:

- Smashing Magazine (category "WordPress": http://wp.smashingmagazine.com/)

- Torque Magazine (http://torquemag.io/)

- WP Tavern (tag "themes": http://www.wptavern.com/tag/themes)

While I like to think the editors of Smashing, Torque and WP Tavern do their best to verify the themes and developers they promote, I would high recommend you *always* scan your free themes for malware and other problems immediately after you download them. We'll go over this in chapter 6.

A good way to find bad or compromised themes (seriously, do NOT do this):

All you need to do is perform a web search for "free WordPress themes" (no quotes.) You will see dozens, if not hundreds, of places to get free themes from. Awesome, right? Well, not so much.

Some of these places are there for the sole purpose of getting you to download a theme that has links to pharmaceutical or porn sites embedded in it (known as Black Hat SEO.) It can get worse with some themes including malware that downloads crap to your visitors' computers, or opens backdoors to your website. You don't want either of these situations.

> **Learn more about free themes:** Read this amazing "ultimate guide" on the evil and shady ways people are using "free" themes to hurt your site, your SEO, and your visitors: http://premium.wpmudev.org/blog/free-wordpress-themes-ultimate-guide/

Truth be told, not all websites with the sole purpose of giving away free WordPress themes are bad. But, you need to know that there are a growing number of them that are evil. It's a classic "pig in a poke" scam where you think you go to buy/get a certain thing, didn't look in the bag, and later found out you got something of lesser value, or worse. Many of these sites are preying upon your trust in the WordPress name to give away compromised themes that inject malicious code into your website. As we learned earlier, WordPress does not inspect and approve every theme out there—just the ones in the WordPress Themes Directory. Always open the bag: always scan your themes. We'll go over this in chapter 6.

> **Ask yourself this:** If there is a huge website, with hundreds of themes, *all* being given away for free, how are they making money? The ads on the site's pages? Not likely. The themes aren't the product, *you* are the product in that they likely want access to your website. As the saying goes: there is no such thing as a free lunch, especially hundreds of free lunches.

What about the developers?

As we have learned in chapter 1B, themes are built by developers. And I'd estimate 99% of themes are built by people who don't work directly for WordPress. Many developers sell themes in marketplaces, and or as work for hire, while some also give them away for free as working samples of their skills hoping to get more work from it.

When you come across a website of a developer giving away one or two themes as samples of their work, I highly recommend checking them out. One benefit to going this route is that it's possible that far fewer people are also using that theme. A possible drawback to this is that the theme may not be actively maintained, in that they built it and posted it to their site but it's not a top priority for them. If you like one of their themes, feel free to ask them if they are actively maintaining it so you can know what to expect.

How to properly shop for free themes (outside of the WordPress Themes Directory)

While I still think it is best to stick to the WordPress Theme Directory for free themes (or get them straight from developer's websites), the call of the free theme may be too strong for you to deny. So, let me take a moment and help you do it properly.

Before you go stomping around in the uncharted waters of websites touting "free WordPress themes" make sure you have a good, up-to-date anti-virus program running on your computer. Some of these websites are using the search term "free WordPress theme" as link bait hoping to spread malware to visitors' computers. Plus, I *highly* recommend you run a virus scan on any theme package you download to your computer.

You will likely shop for a free theme much the same way you do for premium themes (see "How to shop for premium themes" section above.) The difference is that you may not come across many sites that have previews/demos for you to test drive a free theme. Since they are not making money off the themes, they typically keep the marketing efforts to a minimum.

Scared yet? Don't be. Just be cautious and very discerning about the sites you download themes from. In chapter 6 we'll talk about how to check your new theme for hidden problems using a couple plugins.

So, in short:

1) update your anti-virus program on your computer (we talk more about this in chapter 4)

2) shop for a free theme much the same way you do for premium themes (see above)

3) have your anti-virus program scan all downloaded themes before you install them to your server

4) be sure to read the "What not to install" section of chapter 6 *before* you activate your new theme

Pros of free themes (from the WordPress Theme Directory):

- **Cost:** Well, we don't need to go into how a theme being free is a real benefit, do we? :)

- **Availability:** Free themes vastly outnumber premium themes on the WordPress Theme Directory. In fact, as a whole it is probably easier to stumble across free themes than premium ones.

- **Faster:** Since you don't have to mess with the purchasing of a theme we can remove the whole process of an online store and having to get your credit card out. Also, the whole tedious process of signing up for an account is usually gone (though some may make you sign up in order to get a free theme.)

- **Review process:** The WordPress Theme Review Team reviews the themes that are submitted to the Directory before they are available to download. The review process is quite extensive and can be found here: http://codex.wordpress.org/Theme_Review

- **Support:** Every theme from the Directory comes with a support page. If the developer is listening to the questions posted to the Support pages, they can work with you to get your issue resolved. Whether the developer is responsive or not, at least the community can respond to help you get your issue solved.

Cons of free themes (from the WordPress Theme Directory):

- **Features:** You may find that there are fewer feature-rich themes to choose from. And, if your website is on WordPress.com, you will not be able to supplement those features with a plugin or three.

- **Less documentation:** The themes that come from the Directory do not have set up instructions and documentation anywhere near as robust as you will find with premium themes. Many of these are simply a short text document with no real instructions at all.

- **Support:** Support is not mandatory for themes in the Directory. Before you use a theme, see if the developer is active in the Support threads by visiting the WordPress Theme Directory (http://wordpress.org/themes/), searching for the theme by name, and while on the theme page looking for the green "View support forum" button. Look for topics that are labeled "resolved" as well as reading through a few topics to gauge the responsiveness of the developer.

Pros of free themes (from other websites):

- **Cost:** Again, it's free!

- **Documentation:** In some cases, documentation and setup instructions may be far better than the ones from the WordPress Theme Directory.

- **Availability:** Free themes are quite easy to find with a simple web search.

- **Faster:** Since you don't have to mess with the purchasing of a theme we can remove the whole process of an online store and having to get your credit card out. Also, the whole tedious process of signing up for an account is usually gone (though some may make you sign up in order to get a free theme.)

Cons of free themes (from other websites):

- **Cost:** I bet you didn't think I was going to repeat that one, did you? But, it's true: the cost involved with getting a compromised theme can be staggering. Loss of data, loss of SEO, loss of visitors when they see a warning come up in their browser saying your website 'may harm their computer.' To help protect against this read the "What not to install" section of chapter 6 *before* you activate your new theme.

- **Increased Risk:** I pretty much hammered home the multiple risks involved with free themes in the paragraphs above.

- **Support:** You can expect wildly varying levels of support for free themes from "no support" to fully supported, and even offering a tiered paid support structure.

The last word on using free themes

Seriously: stick to the WordPress Theme Directory, or get themes straight from reputable developers. Avoid sites dedicated to just giving away free themes.

A Boilerplate Theme

Where to find a boilerplate theme

As we learned in chapter 1B, boilerplate themes are also called starter or developer themes, and are typically for developers to use to start with when they are creating a custom or full-custom theme. It is unlikely that you will ever download a boilerplate theme and use it as is—though the Bones (http://themble.com/bones/) and Roots (http://roots.io/) themes are usable out of the box, just very stark.

Boilerplate themes typically come directly from the developer(s) that work on it. Like the two examples I linked to above, in virtually all cases the developer will create a site dedicated to the theme. Some post it on GitHub for the community to collaborate on.

Boilerplates are almost never seen in marketplaces like ThemeForest since their audience is likely not looking for a theme that needs further development work. Another reason is that some marketplaces have rules or guidelines for themes aimed to help end-users get a full-featured theme that works out of the box. The very nature of a boilerplate is driven by the technology to help the developer (WordPress Core; servers; browsers; new features of HTML5, CSS3 and APIs,) not to ensure a website owner gets every bell and whistle.

How to shop for boilerplate/starter themes

Do a web search for "WordPress boilerplate theme" or "WordPress starter theme" (no quotes.) If you compare your results to a web search for "free WordPress themes" (no quotes), you should see a big difference in how they are presented. Boilerplates are presented by developers for other developers and focus on the technology. Search results for free themes read like ads for some shady, back-alley used car lot.

When it comes to boilerplates, I recommend first reviewing the following four boilerplates. At the time of writing, they are actively maintained and very solid themes to start with:

- **Roots,** by Ben Word — http://roots.io/ A very advanced and powerful boilerplate that I personally used during the development of a handful of custom themes. I found this to be very SEO friendly and one of the most actively maintained themes around.

- **Bones,** by Eddie Machado — http://themble.com/bones/ I've used this theme as much Roots, and have found it to be very easy to work with.

- **_S,** by Automattic — http://underscores.me/ Pronounced "*Underscores*", this theme is brought to you by the fine folks at Automattic who also brought us WordPress.com and who contribute to WordPress.org. This is a very stark boilerplate, and may be too stark for some developers.

- **Basis,** by Josiah Spence — http://codecarpenter.com/freebie/basis-a-wordpress-boilerplate-theme/ This is one I have yet to use in production. It does however go a little beyond boilerplate in that it includes Facebook Open Graph meta tags (something I leave to SEO plugins), the FitVids.js plugin (for responsive video embeds), and the debatable idea of using "no IDs, only classes" in the markup.

Whether you use one of the above four themes or some other one, you need to start off by knowing what you need (or want to avoid) so you can start off with the right one. Here are few things to think about:

- Do you need a boilerplate with zero- or minimal-styling? There are boilerplates that come with very basic styling to get the party started. Some developers may find that even minimal styling is too much, though depending on the project I feel it can help speed up development time.

- Do you prefer using CSS preprocessors such as Sass or LESS? Some themes, such as Roots, come with LESS files, others just have the compiled style.css file.

- Do you need (or want to avoid) a specific CSS framework, such as Twitter

Bootstrap?

- Do you need to hide the fact you are using WordPress from your source code? (Check out Roots for this.)

- Do you need Facebook Open Graph, Twitter Cards, or microdata/microformats baked into the theme? While I believe the first two should be controlled using the Yoast SEO plugin (so it can be easily updated), the latter is up to you. I prefer greater control by hand-rolling my microdata/microformats into the theme, but there are some plugins to help you out.

If the four boilerplates above don't work for you, a web search for "WordPress boilerplate theme" or "WordPress starter theme" should net you plenty to review. While I tell you not to do a web search for 'free' themes, I feel comfortable doing so with boilerplates. The target audience for these types of themes is developers, making it a bit tougher to get malicious code through. 'Bad guys' are looking for an easy target that has little to no experience finding out the theme is compromised.

> **Scan it all:** While I love the work that went into the four themes above, and that I have faith they are made by competent developers, I still scan every theme I download regardless of who made it. I highly recommend you get in the habit of scanning everything before you upload it to your website. The ten seconds it takes to scan a file beats the hours or days it takes to clean up a website. See chapter 6 for ways to scan a theme.

Pros of boilerplate themes:

- **Cost:** Free! I have yet to find one that you have to pay for.

- **Saves time:** Some boilerplates really give a developer a huge jumpstart, and clear up many common problems that arise across different browsers and devices.

- **Developer documentation:** They often also come with documentation in the code specifically for helping developers right where and when they need it.

Cons of boilerplate themes:

- **Not for everyone:** While some boilerplates can come with a bit of minimal styling, they are typically not ready for a production website. Page layout, widgetized areas and other structural elements are often left up to the developer and designer. You also have to know how to code PHP, HTML5, and CSS in order to modify them.

- **Steep learning curve (sometimes):** Some advanced boilerplates like Roots can really take theme development to the bleeding edge. This may also mean you (the developer) having to learn some new tricks. Again, in the case of Roots, they have a theme wrapper, a custom navigation menu walker, a plugin that allows you to use root relative URLs, and more. While I don't necessarily think of these features as a con, per se, know that they can lengthen the learning curve, eating up some development time on the first go around with it.

- **No updates:** By the very nature of being a starter or boilerplate theme, you will be getting in deep with the code and customizing it to suit your needs. Once you do that there is no updating the boilerplate since (in the vast majority of cases) you will not be able to separate the code you wrote from the boilerplate. At this point you update the custom theme you made as needed, whether or not the boilerplate gets updated.

The last word on boilerplate themes

Review and download 3-5 boilerplates before you start work on one. Open up the files an look at all of them to compare how they are structured. For my level of knowledge in PHP, I found Roots to have a steep learning curve, while Bones was much easier for me to get into.

Some boilerplate themes may handle includes and template files very differently from what you are used to. Some may even handle file storage differently. In the case of Roots, it uses an "assets" folder to hide the telltale default wp-content folder from URLs (when using the root relative URL plugin.) With a little additional work you can effectively hide all traces of WordPress from the source code, if you need to.

Read the documentation for the boilerplate theme you plan on using *before* you start. Again, in the case of Roots there are some timesaving techniques and best practices that the developer has built into the theme.

A Full-Custom Theme

Custom themes don't really exist in marketplaces. They are designed and developed to your specifications, and can take anywhere from a couple weeks to a few months (or longer) to deliver. In this case you are essentially looking for a developer, not a theme *per se.*

How to find a custom theme developer

Finding a developer that can deliver a custom theme takes time. While you can buy, download and install a theme from a marketplace in the matter of a few minutes, finding the right developer can take weeks or months. I'll go over some tips on how to get the right one.

Know what you need before you start. Chapter 2 covers much of what you should have answered before you start looking for a theme developer. Some developers may have additional questions, but going into it with the chapter 2 questions sorted out can really speed up the process. It will also show the developer that you have thought this through and are more serious about the project than someone just asking "how much is a theme?"

You will be using the chapter 2 answers to help build your request for proposal (RFP). But, let's put the breaks on right there and mention that an RFP should NOT be the first thing you send a developer. Reach out to a developer or agency and

1. ask if they are accepting new work/clients

2. give them a three sentence summary of what you need (*not* a timeline of when you want it completed)

> **Example email:** *"Hello Jessica! I found your website while doing a search for WordPress theme developers and I really liked what I saw in your portfolio. Are you accepting new work/clients?*
>
> *If so, I am looking for a WordPress theme that has space for an 'About us' section/page to help establish the owners as being knowledgable, industry professionals. It also has an online storefront to sell skating goods, including being able to showcase, describe and categorize them. And a blog, too.*
>
> *I would love to talk with you about designing and developing my custom WordPress theme."*

Finding a reputable developer. Since the bulk of your research may be online, you will need to be resourceful and cautious. Start with what you know by asking friends and colleagues for leads on developers they have used. Then work your way outward by using your connections on LinkedIn, Facebook and Twitter (which may be tricky for some of you if you don't want your previous developer or customers to know you are making a new site.)

My favorite suggestion is WordCamp, a worldwide meet-up for WordPress users and professionals. Here you can find people—designers, developers, owners and operators —who are passionate about WordPress. Not only will you learn a great deal more about WordPress, but you will be able to meet developers face to face. Check out the WordCamp website to find the next one in your area: http://central.wordcamp.org/schedule/

If that didn't net you a developer, your other option is a web search, and then reaching out by email or phone. Like searching for a theme, how you go about it is important. I'll run you through a typical search for a WordPress developer:

1. Search for "custom WordPress theme development". Or add your city if you are looking for someone local: "custom WordPress theme development Chicago" (without the quotes)

2. Scroll through the list and look for details and URLs that are obviously a freelancer, developer or agency. This is where you need to decide if you want to work with a single person or a team. If a single person, then you need to decide if you want to work with a designer that also codes or a developer that also designs (if you are designing the site and asking them to code it, then I would look for a developer, or a developer that also designs.) If you are looking for a team (of two or more people), then look for results that read more like an agency.

3. Now that you have clicked on a link, let's start looking for indicators of a good fit. First, look for signs of life. Does the footer make you wonder if they are still in business (as in it says "© 2005")? Is there a blog with a recent post? Are there recent additions to their portfolio? A Twitter feed that is still active? Does the "Contact" page say something along the lines of 'not accepting new work'?

4. If it looks like they are still in business, peruse the portfolio. No portfolio of work? Hmmm, go back to the search results and find another developer/agency. If they do have a portfolio, look it over to see if they have WordPress themes listed. If so, does it say they designed and or developed them? We are looking for examples of actual work.

5. If the person/agency claims to have designed the theme, does it look good? If

the person/agency claims to have developed the theme, does it have a link to the live site? If not, do a web search for the website name you see in the example and check out the site. Your decision to contact them should not be based on one example. Look for a handful of examples.

6.   Did steps 3-5 make you feel like you would want to work with the person/ agency? Keep in mind that there are thousands of WordPress theme developers in the world. If visiting their site didn't make you feel excited to work with them, then keep looking.

7.   Repeat steps 3-5 until you have a list of about 3-5 developers/agencies you would like to work with. Take notes on each so you can remember their strengths, or possibly ask questions about anything that wasn't clear or that raised any concerns for you.

8.   Now, take your short list and send each an email to ask if they are accepting new work and give them a short three-sentence summary of the project (see example email above.) Hopefully you found 3-5 different developers to reach out to, but know that even though there are thousands of WordPress developers out there getting in contact with one you want to work with (who also wants to work with you) may not always be easy.

Conversations with a developer/agency. When you find a developer/agency and start a conversation with them there are some important topics to cover. Keep in mind that designers, developers and agencies often choose their clients, not the other way around. You may want to work with them very much, but if they feel the project is not something that interests them, or if you come across as a potential pain in the ass, they may say no to your request.

I've been on the receiving end of many emails and conversations asking me to work on projects. The following are tips on how to make those initial conversations successful:

- **The first one is knowing the answers to the questions posed in chapter 2.** You likely will not be sending them the list as you see it in chapter 2, but I would be worried if many of those questions don't come up in the initial conversation. Being able to answer most questions right away really helps keep the conversation moving along.

- **Be honest.** There is no benefit to lying about your current site, the one you want to build, or even the number of people that visit your site.

- **Don't overshare.** Stick to the conversation and try not to bog down the person with tons of information hoping to impress them that you have it. If they ask for A, B and C, just give them A, B and C. Conversely, if you feel that they aren't asking for any information, have a conversation about that or find another developer.

- **Don't be too rigid.** There are likely things that are really important to you, such as a Twitter feed, an events calendar, or the ability to properly charge Canadians tax when they purchase goods from your site. Whatever it is, know that every line item should be negotiable. There may be some things that the developer simply cannot do, or feels strongly against implementing. Listen, take notes and compare this to what other developers say (but don't share what developers can or cannot do with other developers. Be professional and keep that to yourself.)

- **You're likely not the only one in the pipeline.** Keep in mind that the developer may have other clients' projects already in development, or a vacation planned. If you go into these conversations with a set list of milestones and dates, you may get a 'no,' even if it's simply on principle. Project milestones and dates should be set collaboratively *after* all the details have been shared. Though, if you absolutely have to launch the theme two months from now, you may want to bring that up early on. But, try and be flexible (aka, realistic.)

- **This is not a game.** Every proposal I have ever received that stated I was 'one of many developers competing for the project' never got a reply from me. Any sane person will be reaching out to multiple developers, and of course you will be selecting the one you like best. There is no reason to mention that unless they ask.

- **Be professional and courteous.** Again, this is not you pointing to a developer and saying "Hey, you there! You'll be doing my website." Like any other service industry, they have the right to refuse to work with you. And even more importantly, you are going to be working closely for the next few months or so on what is arguably a very important part of your brand/business. Conversely, if they aren't professional and courteous to you, don't work with them.

- **Spec work. Hell no.** Spec work (or speculative work) is where you ask the designer/developer to do some work for free to 'see if they are a good fit' before hiring them for the project. It's really a design contest of sorts, so please do not ask a designer/developer to do this. You wouldn't ask a plumber or a lawyer to do spec work, so don't think the design/development community should be treated any different. This practice is a blight on the community and needs to stop. And for my designers/developers out there: you can help us all out by refusing to do spec work. If that rant isn't enough, even AIGA is against spec work: http://www.aiga.org/position-spec-work/

Pros of custom themes:

- **Built to order:** Assuming you find an amazing theme developer, you can get exactly what you want in a Custom WordPress theme.

- **There is only one:** You will have a unique design and structure that is only found on your website. Some aspects of it may look similar to others due to common website design conventions, but for the most part you will be the only one using that theme.

- **Less overhead:** You also get just what you want, not a thousand extra features you will never use and which could cause problems down the road.

Cons of custom themes:

- **Cost:** A custom WordPress theme can be cost prohibitive. In some cases they can cost 20 to 100 times more than a premium theme you buy on ThemeForest for $30. Beware of any custom theme only costing you $99, for it may not be what you bargained for. A good, dependable custom WordPress theme takes more than a few hours to build.

- **No updates:** Like boilerplate themes, there are no periodic updates with these themes. Though, if you are having problems or need a feature added, you could go back to the developer about doing an update.

- **Support may be extra:** It is likely that support from the developer may expire after a few months of delivery. Future fixes, add-ons and changes typically cost extra. Since the WordPress Core is constantly evolving, it is not a viable business model for developers to offer free support for a custom theme forever. If a problem arises a year after the theme was released, you can expect to pay the developer's hourly rate to fix it. (I don't think of this so much as a con, as it is something you should factor in when talking with a developer.)

Pro Tip: I highly suggest you work out a maintenance plan with the original developer. This can be a scheduled monthly or quarterly check-in to make sure everything is working properly and fix any small bugs that crop up. Know that major, unforeseen issues—or anything you broke—could cost extra to fix. I like biweekly or monthly site maintenance, but planning a check up every time there is a major WordPress Core update is wise too.

The last word on custom themes

In the same way that not all "mechanics" can work on all types of vehicles, not all "developers" can work on WordPress themes. You are looking for an experienced "WordPress theme developer."

Don't be afraid to ask about a warranty or the scope of support after the theme is live. There is no industry standard on this, so be sure you are comfortable with what you are getting into. I recommend negotiating at least a 30-90 day post-launch warranty to cover problems with the original code. Do not expect the theme to be covered forever.

Be sure to ask about a maintenance plan with your custom theme. This is where the developer can periodically maintain the theme by logging into the Admin Panel. It might cover the WordPress installation, plugins, security issues, etc.

General Things to Look for in All Types of Themes

Compatibility

Do they claim the theme has been tested to work with the latest WordPress release? If no claim has been given, ask. Or, check the date of the last update for the theme. Visit http://wordpress.org/about/roadmap/ to view when the latest WordPress release was. This isn't a foolproof method, but themes released after the latest WordPress release should indicate that it has been tested with that release.

If the theme hasn't been updated since 3.2 came out (July 4, 2011), don't use it: there may be incompatibilities with the latest WordPress. Anything older than WordPress 3.3 (December 12, 2011) would be my cutoff, and already 2.5 years old! That's 'old' in web years. Do yourself a favor and stay with recently updated themes.

Browser support

Each web browser and each version of that browser treat websites differently. If—through Omniture or Google Analytics—you know that an ancient browser such as Internet Explorer 8 is still being used by more than 20% of your visitors, you will want to make sure your theme supports that browser. If you don't see browser compatibility listed on the theme details page, be sure to ask the developer what browsers are supported.

Before You Install a New Theme

So, now you've downloaded a new theme and are ready to install it. There are just a couple very important things we should do before we can make that happen: verify it is clean and free of malware, and back your site up (which we'll go over in our next chapter.)

WordPress Surgery 101

Not to be all melodramatic about it, but to help you remember this important step we should think of installing a new theme as WordPress surgery. In fact, you are opening up your WordPress installation and replacing a piece of it with a new piece. If you install and activate an infected theme, you could be setting yourself up with some serious problems.

Wash your hands

I cannot stress this enough, but you really should be very cautious about the computer you are using to access your website, be it via the Admin Panel, the cPanel, or using an FTP (file transfer protocol.) I have personally seen a user log into their client's infected WordPress site, do some work, then log into their own WordPress site and end up infecting their own site with the same malware.

The risk of uploading, downloading and transferring infected files can be greatly reduced by using an active and robust anti-virus program on your Mac and PC. They can also protect your computer from key loggers, root kits and myriad other forms a malware that can steal your logins and other information.

If you bought a PC, you may be under a false sense of security in that "it comes with anti-virus protection." But that is not 100% true, nor is it 100% reliable. Some anti-virus software that comes pre-bundled on your new PC expires and stops updating after 90 days (check the paperwork that came with the machine.)

Also, while Microsoft has some anti-virus programs in place, they are woefully inadequate for today's level of threats. I personally recommend Avast, AVG, or Sophos anti-virus programs for PCs, though there are numerous options out there.

If you own a Mac, you are likely under the false sense of security in believing the out-right lie that "Macs can't get viruses." This is more worrisome than a PC user running outdated anti-virus software since you are the new big target and can be helping to spread malware. Thankfully you have an awesome solution that works very well: Sophos Anti-virus for Mac, and it's free. I install this on every Mac I own.

The rise in popularity of the Mac is also making them a bigger viable target for people to write Mac-specific malware. Just do a web search for "Mac malware" or "Mac viruses" and see for yourself.

If you run your site from a mobile device—uploading images, files and other assets to your website from your mobile device—you also need protection from malware. At time of writing, Apple does not allow apps to do system-level scanning for malware on iPads and iPhones, but Android and Windows do.

In all cases:

1) make sure you have an anti-virus program installed and up to date.

2) make sure that you regularly scan your computer for malware. Some anti-virus programs only look for problems during the scan. Sophos is one that is actively scanning all downloads (even during web browsing) in real time, and even every USB drive you stick in your computer.

Now that your computer is clean and protected…

Scan Your Site for Malware and Black Hat SEO

This should be done prior to you switching themes. If your current theme is compromised, and you switch it out with a new theme and leave the old theme on your server, you can still have an exploit in the old theme. Even if you are going to delete the old theme, you need to know if it has been compromised so that you can properly clean up the database. The best way to scan it with Sucuri is when it's activated—before you switch themes.

Ok, I promise this is easy. So easy you don't even need to log into your Admin or cPanel. Just visit Sucuri.net and enter your website's URL into the area labeled "Scan your website for free." After about a minute, you should see a "SiteCheck Results" page that (hopefully) looks like this:

Sucuri SiteCheck

Free Website Malware Scanner

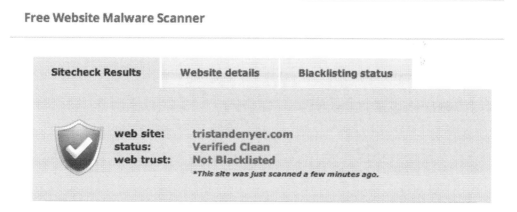

Screen capture of the SiteCheck Results page for Sucuri.net. If there are problems, you will see them listed out below this box.

Anything that is in error, found to be suspect, or a known threat will be listed in red text. Sucuri isn't a company that hides the information and makes you pay to see it—it's all very transparent with Sucuri, even going so far as to list the details and actual code of the threat.

If you find your site has been compromised, I highly recommend you sign up for one of their plans to get your website cleaned up. I have seen a handful of infected and hacked sites get cleaned up by Sucuri in less than four hours, many of them in two hours. Unless you are a professional, cleaning it up yourself can lead to a very long day and possibly a broken website with lost data. Not only that, you might not clean up the back door hackers typically install, so it will just happen again.

Pro Tip: You can scan any website in the world using Sucuri, not just WordPress sites, and not just your own. Meaning, Sucuri is a great tool for scanning websites *before* you visit them. Not every website you visit, but the ones that you feel may be a little suspect. If you are a designer, developer or agency that builds and maintains websites for clients, I highly recommend you take a few moments and have Sucuri scan each of them.

Managed Hosting Protection

If you are using managed hosting, you may already benefit from periodic malware scans by your host. Some managed hosting plans only scan the backup files, others check the production files. Check with your plan to see whether scanning for malware is included, which files they scan, and more importantly, what they do if they find something.

Now that you are cleaned up and the operating room—your computer and website—is ready, let's backup your website so we can start doing some real work!

Backing Up Your Entire Website

While this chapter isn't specific to themes, working with themes means we will be adding, modifying and deleting parts of our website, including the database. Backing up your entire website—database included—will give you piece of mind, and ensure you can take a step or two back when things goes badly.

What Does Backing Up Mean?

To back up your website means to make a copy of every file (WordPress Core, themes, images, and other content) and store it in a safe place for later. To backup your database means to export it as a .sql file and store it in a safe place. Together they are your entire website/blog, and can be used to reinstall a part or all of your website.

Sounds tedious, but the beauty of WordPress is that the WordPress community has made numerous plugins and online services that can do this for you automatically and auto*magic*ally. Depending on the backup option you choose, you can also use your backup file to:

- clone your site and create a development site (such as dev.example.com/)

- migrate your website to a new web host (moving from GoDaddy to HostGator)

- move to a subfolder (from example.com to example.com/blog) or subdomain (from example.com/blog to blog.example.com)

What Are We Looking for in a Backup?

Your specific needs and requirements may vary and expand beyond this, but I recommend three basic things in a good backup plugin or service: it should be scheduled or automatic, it should be secure, and it should copy everything.

Scheduled Backup

I highly recommend scheduled backups since it is not always possible to remember to or even be able to initiate a backup. Depending on the plugin or service you choose, these can be hourly, daily, weekly, or at other designated intervals. At the end of this chapter I tackle the age old question "How often should I backup my site?" This is where scheduled backups will come in handy.

Automatic Backup

This is similar to scheduled backups, but is usually set up to happen only when there has been a change made to your site. If you add an image, change a Post, update a theme, then the backup will initiate and save all the additional and changed files.

Secure Backup

It is imperative that you keep your backup files safe. Your WordPress site contains a couple of very important files that you need to backup, but that can also be used to gain access to your web site, server, and database. One of them is the wp-config.php file in the root of the WordPress Core. It has the login info for the database. The database is the other file that contains even more login info for your Admin Panel. While a seasoned hacker or bot can use a vulnerability to inject code into your site's files without these two, gaining access to these makes it infinitely easier.

We'll go over more security considerations in the following sections of this chapter.

Copy it all

You save little and take a big risk by being frugal with what you backup. I've seen some backup plans only saving the themes folder and nothing else. Another was only backing up the WordPress Core (which includes the themes.) In both cases, the database was being forgotten.

Keep in mind that your database is where the bulk of your content (Pages, Posts, theme settings, comments, users, and more) is stored. Losing that is far more detrimental than losing your theme or WordPress Core.

The last reason you should copy it all was mentioned above in that you can now easily clone, migrate, or move your site as you see fit. (Some backup plans/services have push-button functionality in that you can clone, migrate, or move your site in a matter of minutes from their control panel.)

> **Caution:** Be careful where you store the backup and how you handle it, as everything a hacker needs to gain access to your website and database can be found in this backup.

How Do We Set This Up?

There are numerous options when it comes to backing up your site, but it usually boils down to four types:

- your web host's backup service,

- a WordPress plugin,

- a third-party service

- the manual method

You can use one, some, or all of these. Let's go over each of these options.

Web host plan

Virtually all major web hosting companies have a backup plan. Some offer it for free. Some do it whether you want it or not. And some sell it as an add-on service. Either way, backing up your website using your web host is typically one of the easiest ways to go because there is often nothing to install or maintain. In some cases, you can use your cPanel (control panel) to schedule a periodic backup service or you can initiate one immediately.

Depending on the web host company and the web hosting plan you signed up for, you may even be able to install a backup with a simple click in the cPanel. Others may require you to call their customer service to install a backup. Check with your web host for details about its backup plans.

The backup file may be stored separate from the other files on the website, or in a folder that is not publicly accessible. This can be a bit of a drawback in that the backup may not be accessible to you via the cPanel file manager or even FTP. You may need to ask your web host's customer service for access. It's a better level of security, but (depending on the web host) can be hard to access if you need to.

Managed hosting

The 'other' web hosting option is a managed web host. The vast majority of the managed hosting plans I have seen come with a backup plan as a standard—even mandatory—feature for all sites. Some even scan your backup files for malware, as well as a bevy of other great features. In some cases, managed hosting is less expensive and easier than a handful of other added services you may be paying for already.

WordPress plugin

One of my favorite things about WordPress is the sheer multitude of plugins available. This can also be a problem when you are looking for a plugin and there are dozens of them: which do you choose? (I'll get into that in a minute.)

With a WordPress plugin, you have full control over your backups. Some plugins have a scheduler and the ability to back up only parts of your site or the entire thing, as well as reinstall a backup when you need to. In virtually all cases, you have access to your backup files.

There are so many backup plugins today that I pity the person that has to find one that works for them. So, after trying a dozen of them, and listening to others' experiences, I feel confident in suggesting the following backup plugins. Obviously you should do your own extensive research into each of these before choosing one—these are only suggestions. (And no, I do not have any affiliation with these plugins.)

- **BackUpWordPress** by Human Made Limited - http://wordpress.org/plugins/backupwordpress/ - This really is a simple, free plugin to setup and use. It has a scheduler, the ability to ignore certain folders, and even gives you the choice to backup only the database, only the site files, or both. The backups are stored in a folder inside your WordPress Core, but it uses a unique naming convention for the backup storage folder to keep bots from guessing it. The drawback for some is that reinstalling the backup is a manual process. Another drawback to storing your own files on your own server is that if your server goes down you will lose access to your backups while it is down.

- **VaultPress** by Automattic - http://vaultpress.com/ - Being that this is developed by the very people that operate WordPress, I feel very confident it will be supported longer than any free plugin. And that's the catch: there is a monthly fee to use it. But, seriously, with three tiered plans to chose from, and the fact that they scan your files for security threats as well as help you clean up some common threats, you really should look through their features. A drawback to this is that there is an administrative backdoor to your website in order to backup and reinstall your files. As with homes, any additional door is a security liability. I am sure they do everything in their power to keep the door secure, but it is still a fact that they have direct access. Make your own judgement as to whether or not you are comfortable with a third party having that kind of access to your site.

- **BackupBuddy** by iThemes - http://ithemes.com/purchase/backupbuddy/ - This is another paid service, but my favorite part of this is that you can have your backups sent to your Dropbox, Amazon S3, RackSpace accounts, an FTP server or even emailed to you (though I highly caution you against ever emailing your backups. Email is not a safe place for your backups, *ever*.) You can even reinstate a backup from the dashboard, as well as clone your site to a development server, or vice versa. This is a bit more expensive than VaultPress, so compare the two. Same 'backdoor' drawback as VaultPress above.

- **ManageWP** by ManageWP - https://managewp.com/ - Not only is this a backup service, but it's like the Swiss Army knife for managing all of your individual WordPress sites. As far as backups go, they have a plan that allows you to store your backups on your Amazon S3, Dropbox, or Google Drive accounts. They even have an app for smartphones. It is definitely worth checking out.

If you choose to use a backup plugin, make sure you update it as needed. These plugins deal with sensitive information, so you want to make sure you always have the latest version installed. If you go with a plugin+service like VaultPress, ManageWP or BackupBuddy, make sure the login for your account uses a strong username and password.

> **Multiple websites.** If you operate or manage dozens of websites, the following solution—third-party services—may be easier than having to manage another plugin across all of the sites. (Though, you can use a web app like InfinteWP (http://infinitewp.com/) to manage all of your WordPress sites, themes and plugins from one admin panel. This is slightly different than WordPress Multisite in that it can work across sites owned by different individuals—like clients—and still remain independent.)

Third-party services
In this case I am talking about backup services that do not require you to install a

WordPress plugin, but instead backup your website files and database remotely. This can be done through a remote login into your cPanel, a content delivery network (CDN), or other proprietary means. The takeaway here is that the act of backing up your site is controlled at the server level and in most cases the files are not stored on your server but instead on the company's servers. In the vast majority of cases, no controls or plugin will be integrated into the WordPress Admin Panel, everything is controlled through their website and or a mobile app.

Third-party solutions are often platform agnostic, meaning they don't care if you are running WordPress, Drupal, or have a static HTML website. What matters is typically the type of database you are running —WordPress uses MySQL— and which web host and cPanel you have. As with the VaultPress and BackupBuddy plugins above, you will be granting this company access to your website via your server, so be discerning when it comes to which company you sign up with.

One of the biggest reasons people choose to use a third party service is that it is highly scalable. You can set these up so that every domain and website you add can be managed using one account/application. No plugins to update and manage across multiple sites.

A huge benefit to using a third party will be covered below in "Store backups offsite."

An example of a third-party backup service is SiteVault (http://www.site-vault.com/).

Manual

Lastly, there is the manual method, one of the most secure methods. Don't discount this because it sounds tedious. After reading the options above, you will notice that a common concern runs though them: you are relying on someone else to create a secure and safe plugin/application, and are trusting that they handle your backups properly. One way to ensure things get done the way you want is to do it yourself. It's fairly easy.

All you need is access to your cPanel file manager where you will compress your entire website into a .zip file, then download it to your local drive (or better yet, to your Dropbox, Box, Google Drive or other cloud storage sync folder), and then delete the .zip file from the server. Deleting the .zip file from the server is really important since it contains the wp-config.php file that has your database login information.

> You can also download your entire site via FTP, but be sure you zip the files up first. It can take a long time to download your website one file at a time.

The last step is logging into your phpMyAdmin and exporting your database as a .sql file. Some cPanels allow direct access to phpMyAdmin, whereas other more secure cPanels require you to enter your phpMyAdmin login information (if you don't have it, you can find it in the wp-config.php file in your WordPress Core installation's root.)

With both—site files and the database export—you now have your entire website. What I explained above is essentially what a backup plugin does for you, only they do it much faster and in fewer steps than you can doing it manually.

Why use a manual method? A few reasons may be that you have found plugins, web apps, and web hosts to be unresponsive, have become recently compromised, or are just too expensive. Or, maybe you just love the control that comes with doing the backup yourself.

The downside is that the manual method is for those that have only one or two websites. This is not scalable: you could spend all day manually backing up a dozen websites. Also be aware that since you are downloading a .zip file that can be in the neighborhood of 10MB to over 100MB, it can not only take a long time but it might eat into any data cap your broadband provider or web host has set for downloads.

Store Backups Offsite

In most cases I leave it up to you to determine what is best for you and your site. But with backups I strongly recommend you consider storing them (or at least a copy) offsite. *Why?* Time and time again web hosts experience outages anywhere from a few seconds to a few hours or days.

If the web host's datacenter goes down for hours (like it did with HostGator, BlueHost and HostMonster in the summer of 2013), you may not be able to retrieve any files from your server, let alone a backup. That being said, if a particularly lengthy outage happens—or one you find unbearable—you can get your backup from a third-party that is storing it offsite (and hopefully they aren't affected by the outage too!)

That being said, having a good, reputable third-party store your backups on redundant servers is a smart move. You'll pay for this, but the cost is a tiny fraction of the what it will take to rebuild your website from scratch, or the potential loss in customers/sales should your site be down for hours.

What About Using GitHub As a Backup?

Wait, what is this?

Some developers use GitHub to develop and maintain their WordPress websites. GitHub is a repository for your files that maintains a history of changes as well as version tracking. GitHub allows people to have public repositories ("repos") used for collaboration with other developers, as well as private repos.

This is going to get a bit technical…

You can connect your private GitHub repo to your web hosting account and essentially clone your latest repo for your website to your server using secure shell (SSH). So, how it works is that you make a change to a theme file and save it locally. Then sync it with your GitHub repo, which automatically updates that file on your web hosting account. If I later find out that I totally messed up the site with this change, I can go into my repo and revert that file back to its previous state and re-sync it.

So, how do you back up your site?

This is not a true backup in the sense that it is "version control." Joonas Pulakka's response on StackOverflow says it better than I could:

> *"The fundamental idea of version control is to manage multiple revisions of the same unit of information. The idea of backup is to copy the latest version of information to [a] safe place - older versions can be overwritten."* - Joonas Pulakka, (source: http://stackoverflow.com/a/549621)

If you are comfortable with using your Git/GitHub repo as a 'backup' for your website, then by all means use it. I love using GitHub for my projects and web development, but when it comes to backups I still want to know that I have 5-10 discreet and individual backups standing by, each with a matching snapshot of the database.

What Happens if I Don't Back Up My Site?

Nothing. Millions of people do not backup their websites. Millions of people also get their sites defaced or infected, resulting in lost data, lost customers, lost trust, lost time, lost money… you get the picture. It wasn't fun listening to a website owner cry over the phone when I told her that her website and all its data was gone because there was no backup. Countless hours of work, data and stored documents that she was never going to get back, all because someone deleted the wrong web hosting account. A complete backup (stored on a third-party server) could have had her up and running in under an hour, only losing whatever data was ingested since the last backup.

Do the right thing: periodically back up your site and store it in a safe place.

How Often Should I Backup My site?

I originally wrote this as a blog post for those running a website on a shared server. I modified it slightly for this book and included it below:

These guidelines are aimed at self-hosted websites for individuals, small businesses or other small to medium sized websites using shared web hosting from providers such as GoDaddy, HostGator, Bluehost, or others. Millions of websites fit this bill. If you are in charge of a major brand with household name status, you are likely using a CDN/Cloud from a large web service company and a backup system is in place. The guidelines here are more for the self-hosted websites used by those working with a tighter budget.

How to decide frequency/schedule

We will use some simple math to help estimate how often you should back up your website. After you run through the list, we'll talk about what the total means.

1. You will need to figure out how large your website is (usually in megabytes or gigabytes). For every 50MB of storage your site takes up, +1. So, a 50MB site is +1, a 75MB site is +1.5.

2. You will need to think about how often your site gets updated. Only consider manual updates, such as adding/editing content on pages and posts, additional post comments, or other such conscious edits and additions to your site (a Twitter feed is not a manual update.) Daily is -7, every 3 days is -3, and once a week or month is -1.

3. You will need to research the average *daily* traffic to your site, so, you need to check your site's analytics for this. No guessing! Let's break it down to: 1-500 unique visitors is a +2; 500-1000 is +3; 1000-5000 is +4

The sum total of the three steps above should tell you how many days between backups. A total of zero or less is considered daily (or every other night, if you prefer.)

Example site #1: a 100MB site that gets updated daily (on average) and has 1,050 visitors a day should backup nightly (or every other night.) That's $(2) + (-7) + (5) = 0$.

Example site #2: a 500MB site that gets updated daily and has 4,000 visitors a day should backup every 7 days. That's $(10) + (-7) + (4) = 7$.

This math doesn't make sense!

It's not science, but an estimator to show you how updates, size and traffic should be accounted for in your backup schedule.

I know you are thinking that a site that gets updated daily should be backed up more often, but that is not the case in example #2. For one, the size is 500MB (half a gig!) and the traffic is at a good clip of 4,000 unique visitors daily, so when you initialize your backup your shared server will respond slower and your visitors will experience slower load times (sometimes ridiculously slow, depending on the server.) Do you know how long it takes to archive 500MB of data?* So, this is something you want to do every 7 days, and make sure you do it during off hours for your site. Three a.m. is usually off hours for many sites, but you may want to check your analytics for what day and time has the least visitors historically.

In example #1, the daily schedule is ok since you have a lower visitor count and 100MB shouldn't take too long to archive, even on a slow shared server. But still, you should be choosing a time that is during a period of fewer visitors.

And seriously, I don't expect you to be doing backups manually every 7th or 11th day. You should have access to a good plugin/service for your site that allows you to make a periodic backup schedule.

Caution: Be careful with some cheaper web hosts. Backups can be resource intensive. The last time I initiated a 500MB backup via a WordPress plugin with a site on a cheap, low-budget hosting company, we crashed the whole server. Twice.

Store previous backups

Be sure to store the equivalent of about a month of backups. This way you have a good buffer between when your site had problems (i.e. "got hacked") and when you found out about it. If you backup every night, but don't store more than a day or two back, you have a very short runway to notice you have problems and be able to fix it with a backup. For many users it can take a month or longer to notice you got hacked or lost dozens of pages or were blacklisted by Google. Be aware though that if you backup and store 500MB of data every night for 30 days, you're likely going to go over on your web hosting plan's data cap. Know what your limits are.

No hard and fast rule

It is my belief that 90% of websites on a shared server do not need to backup every night. On the other hand, you do not want to go longer than a month between backups. The bigger the site (in size), the crappier the web host, and the more visitors you are serving all mean you should be backing up less often so as to not overtax the server and show your visitors a slow-loading site.

And yes, some web hosts and third-party services can backup your website nightly with little to no performance degradation (see "Third-party services" section in this chapter.)

Ok, let's install the new theme!

Installing a New Theme

WP For self-hosted situations, installing a theme is step two of a three-step process of swapping out your WordPress theme: 1) download, 2) install, 3) activate. It's also a step that can get a little tricky for some. In fact, there are probably thousands of requests for help from theme developers because the installation caused a "Theme install failed" message.

.COM For WordPress.com situations, you get to skip this chapter since you cannot install a theme. You must choose from one of the themes in the marketplace found in the Themes screen (Appearance > Themes).

What Does Installing a Theme Mean?

It simply means that you are uploading the theme files to your server (we will cover a few ways to do this.) It's also important to note that when you upload a theme, WordPress is going to look for a specific set of files before it will recognize it as a valid theme (a "valid theme" was covered in Chapter 1B.)

If you have purchased/downloaded a theme from a marketplace or website, you will likely get a .zip file during download. Expand the .zip file to see its contents. The image below shows a typical download (from a major theme marketplace) that contains folders for licensing, Photoshop files (PSD), a read me doc, screenshots, and the theme.

A screen capture showing the contents of a typical theme package. In this example, you would upload the "simplefolio.zip" file.

In some cases you will see even more folders and .zip files. In other cases your .zip file may just contain files with .php, .css, and .txt at the end of their names (like what you see on the right above.)

The key takeaway here is that you will need to open/expand the .zip file you downloaded *before* you upload it to your server to ensure WordPress will accept it. In the case above, the "simplefolio.zip" file (center column) is what you want to upload. *Why?* WordPress is looking for files style.css and index.php in order to consider it a theme, and both of these must be the first level of the theme folder (middle column.)

Ok, so you got it? You are looking for a .zip file that has style.css and index.php inside. Photoshop files and other stuff can remain on your computer.

Where Are Themes Installed?

All WordPress themes are installed in the "themes" folder inside the "wp-content" folder of the WordPress Core (../wp-content/themes/). The "wp-content/themes" folder is an inherent part of the WordPress Core. Inside this folder are sub-folders, one for each theme installed, and (hopefully) aptly named by the theme developer so you can identify them.

This is the only place WordPress will look to find themes. If you move theme folders out of this folder, they will no longer be visible in the Admin Panel's Themes screen.

If the theme is active at the time you deleted or moved the folder, WordPress will deactivate it and activate the default theme for the version of WordPress you are running. If the default theme is not found in your "themes" folder, you may end up with a blank white website. Default themes were discussed in chapter 1A.

What Not to Install

You may find that the .zip file delivered by many theme marketplaces is chock full of secondary files like plugins and documentation, tertiary items like Photoshop files, and even non-related items like hidden system files (Mac's .dstore files) or GitHub files (usually .md and .gitignore files.) Worse-case scenarios are themes with malware, viruses and other harmful crap.

Upload just the theme

Only upload the actual theme files, and none of the other stuff listed above. There is little to no value in storing it on your server, unless storing it locally is not an option. If you do have to store these additional files, create a folder in the root directory of your website and store them there.

Scan for malware

While I wish all theme marketplaces were scanning their theme for malware *before* they allow people to download them, this is simply not the case. In fact, I have yet to see any marketplace overtly state their theme download packages are 100% malware, spyware and junk free.

Never upload a theme that you downloaded from a website until you have had your anti-virus program scan it for malware. You should get in the habit of scanning every file *before* you upload it to your website.

Once uploaded, you should scan your installed themes using one or both of the following free plugins *before* you activate them:

- Theme Authenticity Checker (TAC): http://wordpress.org/plugins/tac/ to scan "for malicious or potentially unwanted code."

- Sucuri Security - SiteCheck Malware Scanner: http://wordpress.org/plugins/

sucuri-scanner/ to scan for "various types of malware, SPAM injections, website errors, disabled sites, database connection issues and code anomalies."

Three Ways to Install a Theme

There are three common ways to get the theme onto your server: WordPress Admin Panel, file transfer protocol (FTP), and using the cPanel on your web host. Which one you use is up to you, though the Admin Panel may be the most common method used. We will briefly cover what each means.

WordPress Admin Panel

Your WordPress Admin Panel has the ability to upload theme packages (.zip files), unzip them, and place them in the Themes folder for you. Log in and navigate to Appearance > Themes, then click the "Add new" button at the top of the page, and finally the "Upload theme" button. Click on the "Choose File" button and select your theme's .zip file from your computer. Click on "Install Now" button to upload the file.

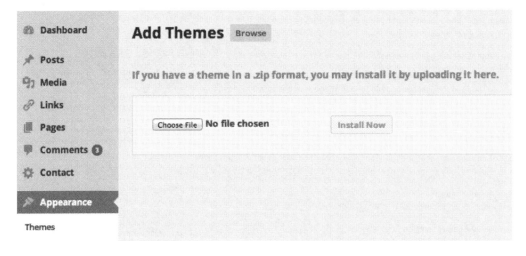

Depending on the size of the .zip file and how fast your internet connection is, this can take a few seconds to a few minutes or longer. At this point, WordPress is uploading the .zip file, unzipping it and inspecting it for properly formatted style.css and index.php files. Upon successful upload and verification, you should see the following screen:

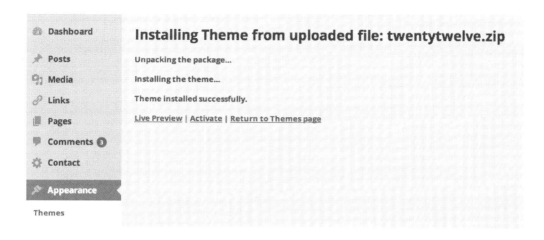

CAUTION: Please read the next chapter "Activating a theme" before you click on the "Activate" link you see here.

Oh crap: If you see a "Theme install failed" message, please see the "Shooting the Troubles" chapter near the end of this book.

You can also install themes directly from the WordPress Theme Directory by navigating to Appearance > Themes, then look for the "Add new" button at the top of the page, and clicking on the "Search", "Featured", "Popular" or "Latest" links. This will allow you to search through the Directory and install a theme directly from there.

Install via FTP

Since there are numerous FTP applications in the world I cannot go over the details for each one. If you are choosing to use an FTP to install your theme, I am going to assume you know how to use it.

Installing your theme via FTP is another option. Keep in mind that this is only placing the files on your server in the "themes" folder. You cannot activate a theme using FTP.

The only real difference with FTP is that you will be unzipping the theme's .zip file to find the theme folder. It's the folder with the style.css and index.php files in it that you want to upload to the ../wp-content/themes/ folder. Unlike the steps in the section above, you do *not* want to upload the .zip file since WordPress will ignore it when it sees it in the ../wp-content/themes/ folder.

Once the new theme's folder is uploaded to the themes folder, check the WordPress

Themes page in the Admin Panel (Appearance > Themes) to see your new theme listed.

> **Oh crap:** If you fail to see your theme listed in the Themes screen, please see the "Shooting the Troubles" chapter near the end of this book.

Install via cPanel

> Many web hosting plans come with some version of cPanel, or at least an admin control panel of some kind. Since there are numerous control panels for all the numerous web hosts in the world I cannot go over the details for each one. If you are choosing to use a control panel to install your theme, I am going to assume you know how to use it.

Similar to FTP above, the main reason you would use a cPanel instead of the supplied uploader in the WordPress Admin panel is because your theme exceeds the max file size limit for uploads.

Once you find the file manager in your web host's cPanel, you need to locate the theme's .zip file (the one with the style.css and index.php files in it) and upload it to ../wp-content/themes/. Once the .zip file is in place, you can use the file manager's "extract" or "unzip" feature to unzip the theme in place. You should now see a folder in ../wp-content/themes/ with the name of your new theme. Check its contents to make sure the theme files are there. Then check the WordPress Themes page in the Admin Panel (Appearance > Themes) to see your new theme listed.

You can, and should, delete the .zip file after you are done extracting it. It is not needed.

> **Oh crap:** If you fail to see your theme listed in the Themes screen, please see the "Shooting the Troubles" chapter near the end of this book.

Pro Tips

Look under the hood

After your new theme passes the TAC and Sucuri tests mentioned above, you can then run the Theme-Check plugin (http://wordpress.org/plugins/theme-check/) to "test your theme for all the latest WordPress standards and practices."

Below you will see a screen capture of a theme that passed. A scan can present action items that are labeled as "Warning," "Required," and "Recommended," as well ones that are simply informative, "Info." A well-built theme will have few or no action items.

Review your scan and make a judgement call on whether you want to proceed using the theme, or contact the developer to see if they are aware of the problems. In some cases, a line item stating the theme is missing support for a 'custom background' may not be of any importance to you. Though, a missing navigation menu might be a deal breaker for your needs.

Running **11947** tests against **Alexandria** using Guidelines Version: **20121211** Plugin revision: **1**

Alexandria passed the tests

Now your theme has passed the basic tests you need to check it properly using the test data before you upload to the WordPress Themes Directory.

Screen capture of a scan using Theme-Check. This particular theme, Alexandria by ThemeAlley.com, passed the test.

Store the documentation for later

In the section above we learned about all the extra stuff that can come with a theme. I highly recommend you store this somewhere you can access later, like a Dropbox account or on your local drive. You'll thank me later.

Low-level bot protection

> **CAUTION:** This tip is only for those of you that downloaded your theme from a marketplace and know you will never update the theme (for whatever reason.) Changing the theme name will remove you from being able to receive theme update notifications, if they are available.

There are people that scour WordPress sites' plugins and themes looking for exploits (like the infamous timthumb.php exploit.) Once an exploitable file is found in a theme (or plugin), hackers deploy bots to make quick work of finding websites using that theme.

How this works is that they already know all themes are stored in the ../wp-content/themes/ folder, so all they have to do is put your domain on the front of ../wp-content/themes/ and the location of the theme's exploitable file on the end, and they have direct access to it. The bot can do this all day, every day, on virtually every website known to man until it finds a match. Then it executes upon that vulnerability and your website is "hacked."

Since the bot is looking for a known theme name, you can rename the folder, re-compress the folder into a .zip file, then upload your theme. So, if your theme's folder is named "awesome-theme" change it to "awesome-theme-1234" by adding something unique to the end of the name. This way your theme's folder is still easy to find in file manager/FTP, but also now sports a unique URL. The bot will be looking for example.com/wp-content/themes/awesome-theme/exploitable-file.php and it will get a 404 error (file not found) and move on.

More detailed information on renaming your theme package and theme can be found in Appendix A "FAQs", section "New Themes: How can I install a theme update as a new, separate theme without overwriting the old theme?"

> **Caution:** Do not rename the folder of an active theme. See next chapter on why this will cause you serious problems.

Stronger bot protection

While the 'low-level bot protection' above is safe to do, the following tip is pretty advanced and can cause issues with some plugins you'll need to be aware of.

You can move the wp-content folder to hide it from bots. Again, the bot will be looking for a known exploit at example.com/wp-content/themes/awesome-theme/exploitable-file.php, but moving the wp-content folder to example.com/assets/ folder will cause the bot will get a 404 error. Do a web search for "how to move wp-content folder" for plenty of tutorials on this.

> **Note:** Know that moving a theme around and hiding it does NOT take care of the fact that it has an exploit. You still need to update your themes and hound developers to fix these problems.

Two themes installed, one activated

I have seen WordPress sites with hundreds of themes installed, and some with five or so installed. Either way, you only need two themes: one that is activated (and it's Parent, if it's a Child theme) and one of the WordPress default themes ("Twenty Fourteen" or "Twenty Thirteen") as a backup theme. If there is ever a problem where the current theme has to be disabled, you will want to have a backup theme to keep your site up and running.

The biggest reason you do not want a bunch of deactivated themes in your themes folder is that one or a bunch of them could contain a known exploit. Even if you've renamed all those theme folders, why would you want to take the risk for a theme that is not in use? If you must keep them, make a copy of them on your local drive, then delete them from the server.

The other reason to remove extra themes is that your backups will be all that much larger for having to backup all those extra files.

No twins

You cannot have two theme folders with the exact same name. Unless you are planning to overwrite an old theme, make sure that any theme you are uploading has a different name than what is already there. Even a "1" at the end of the theme name is enough to be different. Know that, depending on the server, just capitalizing some letters is NOT enough of a difference.

> More detailed information on renaming your theme package and theme can be found in Appendix A "FAQs", section "New Themes: How can I install a theme update as a new, separate theme without overwriting the old theme?"

If you must

If you really, absolutely have to store dozens of your old, unused themes on the server, then use FTP or cPanel file manager to create a new folder in the root directory called "old_themes", place them in there and tell your backup plugin to ignore this folder. You will have to use FTP or cPanel file manager to access them since WordPress will not find them there. But, seriously, keep them off your server.

Back it up!

I will be repeating this statement throughout this book: you should get in the habit of backing up your entire website—especially the database—before you make major changes, additions, deletions to your website. (See previous chapter "Backing up your entire website" for details.)

Activating a Theme

WP This chapter assumes you already have a theme uploaded to your server. If not, see previous chapter.

.COM You already have an unholy ton of themes available for you to activate. You get to activate a theme directly from the marketplace found in the Themes screen (Appearance > Themes).

This Is Your 'Go Live' Moment

You have waded through all the tedious (but necessary) parts of getting a theme, and now you are ready to 'go live' with it. Once you hit "Activate" in the Appearance > Themes screen, your visitors will see the new theme. Are you ready?

Screen capture showing three themes in the Themes screen in the Admin Panel. The middle one shows a hover state revealing the "Activate" button.

When Should I Do This?

This largely depends on your website and type of theme. If you are creating a new website on a new domain name (www.example.com), then don't worry about it: no one is really going to see it since it is new and likely has no visitors. So, you could activate the theme and take the week or weekend to start populating the content. Keep in mind you will be doing this on a live website, so you don't want to drag this out for weeks on end.

If you are swapping out an existing theme for a new one, when you should activate it depends on a couple factors. Does your website have hundreds or thousands of people visiting it every day? How much new content do you need to add to the new theme? If you have a ton of visitors each day and or weeks worth of work getting new content in place, I would highly recommend using a development website and migrate it over when you are ready. Your downtime would be significantly less.

Setting up a development website and migrating it over to your current domain is beyond the scope of this book. A savvy web developer can do this for you, or you can learn how to do it yourself by doing a web search for:

- How to create a WordPress development environment

- How to move WordPress to a different server and web address

> **Teach yourself some pro moves:** An amazing and detailed video tutorial on how to migrate your WordPress website can be found at eduChalk: http://educhalk.org/blog/how-to-move-wordpress-to-a-different-server-and-web-address/

What Does Activating Mean?

So far we learned that purchasing or downloading a theme merely means you are taking possession of it. Uploading it to your website is simply storing it in a folder on your server. But to activate a theme is essentially you saying "this is the look and feel I want my visitors to see on my website/blog."

More importantly, an activated theme is what you are controlling with the Appearance panel's Customize, Widgets, Menus, and Editor tabs. As an admin for the site, this also means that any special widgets, custom fields, and theme management areas that are part of the theme also become available to you in the Admin Panel.

Example: if your current theme has a Widget area called "Expanded footer", you will not see that anymore in the Admin Panel when you activate the new theme. If your new theme has a Widget area called "Twitter feed", you will now see it available in the Admin Panel upon activation of the theme.

What Happens During Activation?

In chapter 1A we mentioned that you must have at least one theme activated for your site to work. And you can only have one theme activated at a time. So, when you activate a new theme, WordPress will deactivate the old theme you were using. This means that all widgets, custom fields, theme management areas ("Theme Options") that were part of the previous theme are no longer accessible via the Admin Panel. The settings and content of those Widgetized areas are stored in the database should you ever need to re-activate the old theme.

For the geeks in the room: when you activate a new theme, WordPress is updating the "template" and "stylesheet" records in the wp_options table in your database. Both of these records are using the name of the folder for your theme. So, if you upload and activate a theme where the developer named the theme folder "FooBar1234", your database will be looking for exactly that name (and it is case-sensitive.) **This is important to know because once you activate a theme, you do not want to rename the folder it is in.**

option_id	option_name	option_value
44	template	twentythirteen
45	stylesheet	twentythirteen
147	_transient_feed_ac0b00fe65abe10e0c5b588f3ed8c7ca	a:4:{s:5:"child";a:1:{s:0:"";a:1:{s:3:"rss";a:1:{i...
180	_site_transient_update_themes	O:8:"stdClass":3:{s:12:"last_checked";i:1377968654...
190	_site_transient_theme_roots	a:4:{s:12:"twentyeleven";s:7:"/themes";s:16:"twent...
191	theme_mods_twentythirteen	a:1:{i:0;b:0;}

A screenshot of the database using phpMyAdmin. Note the option_value lists the theme's folder name, not the Theme Name you see in the style.css header.

> **Caution:** Some (thoughtful) developers will code their themes and plugins to clean up after themselves by deleting all the tables and records in the database that are pertinent to that theme/plugin upon deleting it. Do not delete an old theme until you are sure you have no need for it, and any of the special widgets and custom fields it once controlled. See Chapter 13, Uninstalling/deleting your theme, for more information.

Estimating Time Needed to Complete Theme Setup

So, how do you gauge the amount of work it will take to get the new theme up and running and looking the way you want? Being that there are thousands of themes out there, each with dozens of settings and content areas that are special to that theme, it is impossible for me to give you a solid answer. But here is how you can get a feel for how long it will take before you dive head first:

- Read the new theme's documentation *before* you activate it. Are you ready? Do you have everything it needs? Do you understand what they are asking you to do?

- Review the customer forums for the theme. These are often open to the public, and by reading the latest comments you can get a sense of the developer's support, outstanding bugs, and other problems you may run into. If one exists, it will likely be linked to from the theme's marketing pages (where you found the theme.)

- Review your current website and note all the additional images you will have to create, and any copy you will have to write for any new widgets or features this theme comes with. Getting as much ready as possible before you activate the theme will make for a smooth process.

Things to Watch for

Not all themes are the same. Some of the many things I have seen:

- In one case we were moving from a theme that had the ability to show featured images on blog posts to a theme that did not. The new theme simply did not have it, and we had to create a child theme to add that functionality back in.

- In another case the featured image functionality was used to populate a very wide and thin image along the top of the blog post. The website owner had no feature images set, and the developer didn't plan for there being no feature image, thus showing a giant, ugly black box at the top of the page. (That client chose to spend hours sourcing and uploading and assigning a feature image to all 50+ posts she had.)

- The old theme had its own custom shortcodes allowing for the admin to create columns of text in her Posts and Pages (like a newspaper.) The new theme didn't recognize them and simply displayed them to visitors as they were written: `[column1] blah blah blah [/column1]` She had dozens and dozens of Pages with these column shortcodes on them that took her a week to fix (remove) by hand.

- In virtually all cases, any widgets you had assigned to sidebars or other widgetized areas will be moved to the "Inactive Widgets" area of the Appearance > Widgets screen. This is because the two themes are not the same. Don't worry, moving them to the "Inactive Widgets" is a normal function of WordPress to preserve them. You simply need to drag them back over to the widgetized areas on the new theme. Note that the new theme dictates the placement and amount of Widget areas, meaning, you may have more or less of them and they may be displayed in different places than your last theme.

> **Hide Unwanted Shortcodes:** If you run across the problem stated above where you have tons of unused/unstyled/unpopulated shortcodes, an easy, non-developer way to hide them is using the Hide Unwanted Shortcodes plugin (http://wordpress.org/plugins/hide-unwanted-shortcodes/.) They will remain in the content, but basically be rendered as unstyled, hiding the brackets and names. Any content it wraps around should remain untouched.

And that is just a hint of the snafus I've come across when switching themes in WordPress. The truth is that there will often be no way for you to plan for every little thing that could go wrong or missing, but planning can certainly mitigate your problems. Or, you might not have any problems at all. Here's hoping.

How Do I Turn It Off?

I have had quite a few people get confused over WordPress' choice of words when it comes to "Activate" and "Deactivate". When it comes to plugins, you can do both "Activate" and "Deactivate", but for themes you only get to activate them. As we mentioned in chapter 1A, you can only have one theme activated at a time. All other themes you have installed are deactivated, like in standby status.

So, to 'turn off' a theme, you must activate another theme in the Admin Panel under Appearance > Themes. If you do not have another theme installed, you will need to install a second theme and activate it, which will turn off or deactivate your current theme.

Test Your New Theme

Now that your theme is installed and activated it's time to make sure everything is as you expected. I highly recommend you do this immediately after activating a new theme.

Why Are We Doing This?

To put this in terms of shopping, it is the same as comparing your grocery list against the receipt and checking whether everything is in the bag. Doing this before you get all the way home can save you a trip back to the store at a later date.

If this is a purchased theme, you want to make sure the claims made on the marketing page match up to what you see in the Admin Panel as well as what the visitors see on the public side. As time goes by and updates are made to the theme in the marketplace, it can be more difficult to make a claim that something isn't as it was described when you bought it.

When you are doing this for a client (or working on a custom theme with a developer), it is imperative that what you deliver matches up to the statement of work you and the client agreed on.

> **Old browsers.** Developers would need to add a lot of hacks, fixes and JavaScript into themes to make IE 6, 7, and 8 render some of what the modern web does today. Developers don't always do that since usage for these browsers is typically 10% of visitors or less. If your theme's marketing pages expressly state they support IE 8, expect it to work well in IE 8, but not IE 7 and below.

How to Validate a Purchased Theme

The process can vary depending on the theme, the claims made by the developer/ marketplace, and your content. The following subsections are to give you some guidance on how to verify a handful of (common) features.

If you purchased a theme from a marketplace, revisit the marketing page where you bought the theme. If you don't remember where you bought the theme, there are a few ways to figure it out:

- Check your email inbox for a receipt. Most (good) marketplaces will have a link to the marketing page you got the theme from.

- Do a web search for "WordPress theme [enter theme name here]". You can find the theme name in your Admin Panel by navigating to Appearance > Themes, and look for the name in bold text under "Current Theme" heading. Keep in mind some purchased themes may have the same name as other themes, so double-check the theme page in the search results matches your theme. You can also add the developer's name (hover over theme and select "Details") to your web search to narrow the results. Example: "WordPress Awesome theme by Rad WordPress Themes"

- Look for the stylesheet header in the theme's "style.css" file for a link to theme (or developer) page. A valid theme header will include a "Theme URI" and a "Author URI" (the 'author' is the developer.) You can find this file in your Admin Panel by navigating to Appearance > Editor. "style.css" should be the default file shown on the screen. (If for some reason it is not visible, use the "Select theme to edit" pulldown menu on the top right to select your theme.) In some cases, the "Theme URI" link might only point to the main page of the developer, and not the actual theme page as shown below.

 Edit Themes

Specialist: Stylesheet (style.css)

```
/*
Theme Name:     Specialist
Theme URI:      http://templatic.com/cms-themes/specialist-business-wordpress-theme
Description:    Developed by Templatic Team
Version:        1.0.1
Author:         Templatic
Author URI:     http://templatic.com/
*/
```

Screen capture of the stylesheet header, as seen in Appearance > Editor screen.

Now that you have the features and details promised by the developer open in your browser, open your website and your Admin Panel each in a new tab or window so that you can switch back and forth easily. With these 3 tabs/windows open, you will start going down the list on the theme's marketing page (or in the case of a Custom theme, a statement of work) and checking to see that you have that functionality/feature/option in your Admin Panel and or the website.

The principle idea here is to check to make sure the features and options you needed are actually delivered and working in the theme. Let's go through some of the more common things found in WordPress themes today:

> **Force reload (hard refresh):** When testing, always reload the page by holding the shift key and clicking on the reload icon (or cmd-shift-r) to ensure you are not looking at cached content. Read more: http://www.wisegeek.org/what-is-a-hard-refresh.htm

Dummy Content

Some themes include a file containing 'dummy' or 'sample' content. You can recognize it by opening the theme package and looking for a file with an .xml file extension. They may even be named something like "sample-content.xml".

Importing this will load additional content such as Posts, Pages, comments, and/or categories into your database. The Posts/Pages are often composed of gibberish, but some theme developers use them to show many (or all) of the theme's features. A common example would be a page showcasing all of the shortcodes available in the theme and how their content appears on the screen.

> **CAUTION:** DO NOT upload this dummy content to a website that has real or existing content already in place—in some cases it can overwrite your existing content.

For new websites with no existing content, uploading this dummy content can be an easy way to populate a WordPress website, but I still try to deter people from doing so for the following reasons:

- By walking through the theme's documentation yourself and seeing how your website reacts to your changes you will get a better understanding of what your theme can do and how to correct/edit those features.

- Uploading this content often adds dummy Posts and Pages that display gibberish, fake categories and tags, and other content. These Posts/Pages are often publicly viewable by default, and if you forget to delete them, Google can find them and consider them part of your site's content.

- If you have your menus set to "Automatically add new top-level pages," you could end up adding numerous dummy pages to your menu.

- Lastly, if you plan on using this site for real content, you will have to delete all the dummy Posts, Pages, categories and tags by hand. (Permanently deleting Posts/Pages will automatically remove them from the menu.)

Fonts

Keep in mind that the ability to select from a huge list of fonts is using a technique called *font embedding* where the font files are downloaded to the visitor's browser. This is often used because it is likely they will not have the font the website wants to use on their computer.

Not all browsers support embedded fonts, especially Internet Explorer 7. There is only partial support in Internet Explorer 8. Modern browsers like Chrome, Safari and Firefox do support it. See "Shooting the Troubles" chapter if you are having problems with fonts.

Check for fonts that were promised:

1. **Does the theme's options panel show all the fonts as advertised?** This can be found in the new theme's options panel, which is typically found in the left nav

bar in the Admin Panel. Open the theme options panel (if available) and select a font, then click the save button in the options panel.

2.   **Does the website update to show the font you selected?** View the tab showing your website and reload the page by holding the shift key and clicking on the reload icon (or cmd-shift-r) to ensure you are not looking at cached content.

Font styling: sizes, headings, colors, oh my!

Typically, where there are font choices, there will likely be multiple options for selecting the size of headings and paragraph text, as well as a near-infinite array of colors. Unlike font embedding, all browsers respect virtually all of these values (font size, colors), no matter how old the browser is.

1.   **Does the theme's options panel show all the font styling options as advertised?** This can be found in the new theme's options panel (if available), which is typically found in the left nav bar in the Admin Panel.

2.   **Is it able to be updated?** In the theme options panel and select new values for your headings, body copy and colors, then click the save button in the options panel. (Unless the theme options has a "reset" option, be sure to write down any default values before you change them.)

3.   **Does the website update to show the font styling you selected?** View the tab showing your website and force reload the page. You should now see your new font sizes and colors.

Special skins

Some themes come with a "light" or "dark" skin where with the click of one button you can change the appearance of your theme to use a pre-designed overall appearance. Some have multiple choices, and some even let you further customize the skin through font, color, and background image options. Most browsers should have no problem showing typical skins.

1.   **Does the theme's options panel show all the skins as advertised?** This can be found in the new theme's options panel (if available.) Take inventory of all the skins available in the options panel. Compare to the list of skins promised in the marketing page.

2.   **Is it able to be updated?** Select a new skin, then click the save button in the

options panel.

3. **Does the website update to show the skin you selected?** View the tab showing your website and force reload the page. You should now see your new skin. Compare this to the preview/demo of the skin on the theme's marketing page. (If it doesn't have a preview/demo, shame on them. Seriously.)

Sliders, slideshows, slide decks, carousels...

Almost all themes come with a slider (also called a slideshow, slide deck, carousel, rotator, etc.) Some are now shipping with more than one option of slider. But know that not all sliders will work on all browsers. Some of the more modern sliders using HTML5 and CSS3 *may* not work properly on (you guessed it!) Internet Explorer 8 and older. At time of writing, IE8 is still being used by about 10% of users globally (which is still millions of people and companies.)

> **Caution:** Some developers make you purchase a slider license or plugin in order for certain sliders to work. Credible and ethical developers will mention this in the marketing copy before you purchase the theme.

1. **Does the theme's options panel show all the sliders as advertised?** This may be found in the new theme's options panel, if available, or in a separate tab specifically for sliders (see your themes documentation for location.) Take inventory of all the sliders available in your theme. Compare it to the list of sliders promised in the marketing page. If you see any that are missing, reread the marketing page (or theme's documentation) to make sure you are not expected to install a plugin to get it to work.

2. **Is it able to be updated?** (If you have more than one slider option) select new slider type. Depending on the type of slider, you will likely need to refer to the theme's documentation for how to set it up and add content to the slider (many don't work without manually adding content.) Then click the save button in the options panel (or plugin, if required.)

3. **Does the website update to show the slider you selected?** View the tab showing your website and force reload the page. You should now see your new slider. Compare this to the preview/demo of the slider on the theme's marketing page. (If it doesn't have a preview/demo, shame on them. Seriously.)

Shortcodes

Shortcodes are short bracketed terms that are content placeholders. They get converted/processed by the theme to render specific content such as galleries, Twitter posts and feeds, sliders, contact forms and a million other uses.

Asking Admins and Editors to use short codes is easier than asking them to paste in a bunch of code into the editor each time, plus, for the developer, they keep the feature's code consistent and easier to maintain. They are typically formatted like this `[shortcode term here]`, but some can also include variables to modify the shortcode's function like this version for the RoyalSlider plugin `[new_royalslider id="1"]`. Some themes add the ability to get/paste in shortcodes from the WYSIWYG (What You See is What You Get) editor while writing Posts/Pages, while others require you to refer to documentation and cut and paste them in.

Depending on the actual code and functionality behind the shortcode not all browsers may support it. If the feature/functionality is HTML5 and CSS3 dependent (like a slider/slideshow), Internet Explorer 6, 7 and 8 might not render it properly.

> **Shortcode Pages:** If you loaded the 'dummy content' that is often included with new themes (I do not recommend this! See beginning of this section,) then you might already have a page called "Shortcodes." This will likely show you a Page using many or all of the shortcodes the theme makes available to you. Viewing this Post/Page in your Admin editor and selecting the "Text" tab on the WYSIWYG editor will reveal the actual shortcodes' formatting, for example `[shortcode id="1"]`. Again, your theme's documentation will tell you if you can use the WYSIWYG editor to insert shortcodes or if you need to cut-n-paste from this page.

1.   **Does the Post/Page WYSIWYG editor (or documentation) show all the shortcodes as advertised?** Take inventory of all the shortcodes promised by the developer on the marketing page. Compare to the WYSIWYG editor, if available, or documentation.

2.   **Is it able to be updated?** Open an existing Page/Post (or create a new one) and select a shortcode from the WYSIWYG editor (or documentation), then click the "Update" button in the edit panel. Note that "Previewing" a page is not always accurate, and may not always load shortcodes or certain embedded content such as video or social media widgets. Sometimes "Update" is the only

way to truly check how a Post/Page will appear to your visitors.

3. **Does the website update showing the shortcode you selected?** View the tab showing your website and force reload the page. You should now see the shortcode's output. Compare this to the preview/demo of the shortcode on the theme's marketing page. (Again, if it doesn't have a preview/demo, shame on them. Seriously.)

Responsive layouts

Many of the themes today come with the inherent ability to auto*magic*ally adjust the layout for viewing on various screen sizes. The layout resizes, and elements on the page can rearrange themselves to fit better for smaller screens. Some themes allow the visitor to select to view the webpage in a "desktop" or "fixed width" format by clicking a link (usually in the footer.) Some themes allow the Admin to turn off the responsive feature meaning all users see the "desktop" layout.

To test the capabilities of your new responsive theme, grab a modern smartphone, tablet and a laptop/desktop computer. Load the website on each device. In each case, you should be able to comfortably read the text without needing to zoom in/out. You should also be able to see everything on the page without scrolling side to side (unless horizontal scrolling is part of the theme design.)

Images and video should also resize to fit the viewable area, not spill off the screen. It is up to the developer to add specific CSS and JavaScript to help (technically "force") images and video to resize for smaller screens. A well-coded theme will even override the specific size values applied to all images in WordPress, and can even force YouTube and Vimeo videos to respect a responsive layout.

> **Video support:** In today's world of themes, there is no reason to purchase a responsive theme that cannot do responsive images and YouTube videos. Bonus points for embedded Vimeo videos, but seriously, in my opinion they should be responsive too.

- **Does the theme respond to the size of the screen?** Bring up your website on a smartphone, then turn it from portrait layout (vertical) to a landscape layout (horizontal.) Did the site and all of its contents resize to properly fit the screen without having to zoom out/in? Note that Flash objects and Flash based video will not render on Apple phones and tablets, and some Androids. On tablets, you may see the 'desktop' layout in the landscape orientation and a smaller responsive layout when in portrait. This behavior is normal and common. On your laptop/desktop computer, grab the corner of the browser window and resize it smaller/larger. Some responsive themes update as it resizes, some only refresh after the screen stops moving.

- **If the theme has a "desktop version" link, does it work?** Look for the link in the footer of your website. Not all themes have this feature, but if yours does you should try it out. Clicking it is not permanent, you can switch back.

- **How about them tricky little buggers?** Ok, these are some nitpicky items. But they do crop up in websites I visit and I know most can be fixed with a little CSS. Nearly all theme marketing pages will never make mention of these fixes, but I look for them anyway. Why does it matter? In some cases these problems can actually break the format of a responsive site and make it render a little odd on small screens, especially:

  1) Create a new Post/Page and add the following items: a very long URL as text and make it a link—you can find a long URL in your address bar every time you do a Google or Amazon search.

  2) create a bulleted list of about 4-8 items.

  3) insert a Twitter post ("tweet") by pasting in the tweet's URL—you can get details on how to do this here: http://en.support.wordpress.com/twitter/twitter-embeds/

  4) insert an image with a caption of about 10-15 words.

  5) Nested comments. This is tedious to set up, but worth it. You basically just keep replying to your own reply. Find/create a comment on a Post/Page, then reply to it. Now reply to your reply and do that a total of about 4-6 times.

- Once these (and any other page elements you want to test) are in a Post/Page, visit them on a modern smartphone, tablet and a laptop/desktop computer to see how they render. Long URLs can break out of the container they are in and just keep going (too bad too, since they are a simple fix using "word-break," "overflow-wrap" and or "hyphen" in the CSS.) For the rest of the items, just take a look to see if they respond to small screens in a way that is ok with you. If they bust up the design too much (it will be obvious to you), or just look horrible, take a screenshot and contact the developer that built it. They might update it in a future release.

And the Rest…

The above six features are only covering a fraction of what developers are commonly stuffing (err, I mean "offering") into themes today. I chose to focus on these because they are some of the problem areas I commonly see people run into. Much of this is because older browsers don't support HTML5 and CSS3, which many of the above features rely on.

Be sure to read a theme's marketing page to see what browsers they do support. Make sure the theme you select aligns with your website's customer base so you get the proper support (I covered this in chapter 3.)

I highly suggest you test out all of the features of your new theme before you deliver it to your client, or deploy it publicly. You can do this by installing and activating the theme on a separate domain that is not for production (known as a "development" or "staging" site) before activating it on your actual or production website.

Compare the Theme To Your Features Checklist

Grab the checklist I had you make in chapter 2. Before you start to add any content and get waist deep into this theme, make sure it satisfies your needs. It's one thing that you verify your theme works as advertised. It's a wholly different animal that the theme actually delivers on the features you/your client deemed necessary before undertaking this search for a theme.

Sometimes You Need a Plugin

Some features can be added using a plugin, so be sure to make a list of features or items lacking in the theme so you can seek out a plugin that completes the feature set you need (see chapter 3.)

Setting the Baseline

When working with clients, I like to take a snapshot of the website I delivered. I can do this by making a complete backup of the new website (example.com) and installing it on a subdomain of their site (dev.example.com). Since this will not get updated by the client, it gives me the ability to look back and see what the site looked like and how it behaved when I last delivered it.

Not everyone has the ability to do this, so another option is to take a screen capture of the website. This is not as ideal since you cannot capture the interactions like hover state or slider behavior. Do a web search for "screenshot website" to see a huge list of available options that can produce an image showing the entire web page, not just the part that is visible.

A more tedious way could be to record your screen as a video while you use the website. Some apps/programs allow you to record your voice so that you can annotate the video as you go.

Either way you choose to do this, you want to record how the website looked during its "known good configuration." This can help you greatly if a client challenges you on what was delivered.

Dealing With the Required and Recommended Plugins for Themes

Now's the time to talk about the plugins theme developers require or recommend you to buy (or download for free) to get the full functionality promised in the theme's marketing pages.

This chapter is intended to be an introduction to required and recommended plugins for themes, and will not cover everything there is to know about plugins (that could be its own book!) My goal here is to address my concerns for themes that require specific plugins in order to work, and to give you a clearer understanding of what you may be getting into when using or purchasing such a theme.

Quick and Dirty Introduction to Plugins

Plugins typically add features and services to a site, though some plugins can remove services as well. They quite literally plug into the WordPress Core, which allows them to control just about anything from the server, to the WordPress Core, to the theme itself. Some plugins can even interact with third-party applications such as Twitter, Dropbox, Instagram, or other web apps and services.

Using the 'house analogy' we started with in chapter 1A, a plugin would be the cable TV streaming 500 channels into your home, a security system to protect the house, or an alarm clock to wake you up every day. To relate that: plugins can reach out beyond your website and bring in content (Twitter, Instagram, RSS feeds), can protect your site from attacks, and can do scheduled tasks such as backup the site or Post content on your behalf.

Plugins can be installed and activated via the Admin Panel's Plugins screen, and since they are typically independent of each other and the theme, they can be removed without damaging the WordPress Core or the theme's files. Again, removing a plugin works as though you were removing an alarm clock from your home: the cable TV still works and the security system is still going strong. The only thing that changes is you might end up late for work.

In the same vein, you can switch out your theme and the plugins remain installed and activated. All the data you add and settings you make for a plugin is stored in the database and can be used with any other theme that supports that plugin.

> **CAUTION:** Not all plugins work on all themes. Some plugins require a theme to include particular snippets of code, others require the theme to be structured a certain way, and then there are some that might conflict with scripts in the theme.

In short, required and recommended plugins for themes are a developer's way of saying "these work!"

Embedded Plugins

Earlier we mentioned downloading and installing a plugin. This is the traditional method of adding functionality to a WordPress website, and one that I prefer. But, some developers choose to embed popular plugins *into* the theme (i.e. copying the plugin's code into the theme files.) So something that was once able to be added and removed by the website owner is now integral to the theme and cannot be removed.

We will talk more about embedded plugins, as well as their pros and cons, later in this chapter.

What Am I Being Asked to Do?

When you look at the marketing pages for a particular theme and you see something that says "WooCommerce ready" (for an online store) or "bbPress ready" (for a forum) it can mean that the theme is ready to support those plugins being added to the site. In some cases you have to download and install specific WordPress plugins—like "WooCommerce" and "bbPress"—to get all of the functionality that is being offered in the theme's marketing pages.

Other themes use plugins in their demos to show off photo or video galleries because it really helps sell themes. The theme might not have any ability to create that particular gallery, per se, but the documentation may tell you that if you download a particular plugin you could get the same gallery on your site.

The Roots developer theme by Ben Word has a list of recommended plugins for forms, caching, SEO and more. If you didn't install them you would still be able to use the Roots theme as advertised. In this case, he is recommending a list of plugins that help enhance the experience of the site for the owner and the visitor. This is a different than some marketplace themes that built a major feature around a plugin expecting you to install, and possibly pay for the required plugin.

Things to Be Wary of

Take a moment to look through the best selling WordPress themes on any major theme marketplace, and you will see a trend: each developer offering scores of sliders, shortcodes, widgets, sidebars, galleries, fonts and on and on. When a new feature hits the WordPress world the next theme developers build (often) includes everything from the previous theme *plus* the new hottest features.

Many of these features come from popular plugins. As mentioned above, some developers go so far as to incorporate the plugin's code into the theme on the pretense of saving you the trouble of having to install the plugin. At that point it is technically no longer a true WordPress "plugin", but a feature of the theme. Now, in order to update the plugin's functionality you have to wait for the developer to update the theme, and for you to update it on your website.

Example: A developer could embed five different slider plugins into the theme, and through the Admin Panel a user could select to use one of those sliders. If coded correctly, the theme would ignore all the code for the other four sliders and only use the one the Admin selected. The problem is that you now have code for four other sliders that you will never use. It's about as useful as having four extra steering wheels in the trunk of your car in case you ever want to swap them out.

Bait and switch

I've also seen this happen: a theme claims X number of sliders, and even shows you a live demo of them all working. You buy the theme and find that one of the sliders is a "premium feature" and requires you to buy the plugin or pay a licensing fee to use it.

It starts to get a little shady when the theme developer fails to mention that a certain feature requires an additional paid (also called "premium") plugin. Some required plugins are free, but some can cost anywhere from $3-30 or more, and some can incur a monthly fee. Be sure to read all of the marketing copy, and if you feel you were later asked to buy a plugin to gain all of the functionality of a theme without mention of it in the marketing copy up front, contact that theme developer directly*.

The true bait and switch comes in to play only if the theme developer fails to mention that a certain feature requires a "premium" plugin they profit from. Let's say they show a really nice slider with some marketing copy talking about how awesome this slider is and how it makes coffee for you in the morning and solves world hunger (you know, really pouring it on.) You go to buy the theme, download it and then find out in the documentation you have to also buy the "premium" slider plugin, and lo and behold the developer has an affiliate link for that plugin! He/she is getting a cut of that sale for "referring" you. In some cases they are selling it themselves.

Theme developers and marketplaces should tell you up front which features require premium plugins you must buy in order to make the theme work the way you see it working in the demo, or as touted in the marketing copy.

*If you feel the theme you received is not representative of the one described in the marketing or shown in the demo, take these steps, in this order:

1) Be sure that you have thoroughly reread the marketing copy and documentation that came with the theme.

2) Contact the theme developer directly (via email or their forum, if there is one.) Keep your message professional, explaining why you feel the theme is not like the one described or shown in the demo. There may be an easy fix, misunderstanding or explanation for it. Give them up to 3 days to reply before moving on to the next step.

3) If the theme was sold through a marketplace, contact the marketplace directly. Tell them you reached out to the theme developer and have not received a response. Give them up to 2 business days to reply before moving on to the next step. If the theme was sold directly by the developer, try reaching out to them via other channels, such as their Twitter feed or Facebook page. While you are on their Twitter/Facebook pages look for signs of life—have they posted in the past month or two?—and look for any messages saying they're

taking a vacation.

4) If a couple weeks or more has gone by without any response, you may be out of luck in getting it fixed and resorting to requesting a refund via your payment provider. Major marketplaces like ThemeForest, WooCommerce and Elegant Themes should get these types of issues resolved in the matter of days (if not hours.) But, with the numerous places selling themes today, you may run into a few smaller ones with little to no customer service. I hope this doesn't happen to you.

The right way: Pippin Williamson's Easy Digital Downloads marketplace is a good example of how to offer and sell premium themes and plugins to users. First, you can buy and use the themes without the premium plugins he sells. Secondly, the plugins (called "extensions" here, since they depend on his free Easy Digital Downloads plugin) are marketed and sold on his site next to the themes, all out in the open.

 Dashboard

This theme requires you to install the Yoast Wordpress SEO plugin, download it from here.

This theme requires you to install the Disqus comment system plugin, download it from here.

This theme requires you to install the Wordpress Popular Post plugin, download it from here.

Above image is from Paul Lund's post "Alert Theme Users To Required Plugins" recommending developers to alert users of required plugins in the Admin Panel: (http:// www.paulund.co.uk/theme-users-required-plugins)

What Happens if I Don't Install the Plugins?

Carefully read the marketing copy and the theme's instructions to see if any plugins are "required" or "recommended." There's a big difference between the two.

In the case of "recommended" plugins, nothing. Ben Word's Roots developer theme marketing page has a list of recommendations to help you with managing SEO, faster page loading, customized forms. If you don't install them, you simply don't benefit from those plugins.

In the case of "required" plugins, a couple things may be at stake. First—like with recommended plugins—if you choose not to install the required plugin, your theme will not have that functionality. Second, if your new online store theme specifically requires you to install the WooCommerce plugin in order to work, you might not be able to use another ecommerce plugin for that theme. Some themes are developed specifically for plugins like the WooCommerce plugin, and using another may pose layout problems or fail to deliver on the full functionality the theme developer intended or claimed.

Pros and Cons of Doing Themes This Way

Pros of using a plugin

- The top of my list is the fact that decoupling plugin functionality from the theme (more specifically: not putting it in the theme in the first place) allows you to get the proper and direct support for any issues you are having with the plugin. Some theme developers might not know anything about the plugin code and would not know how to support you if a problem arises. For plugins embedded in themes, theme developers often defer to the original plugin developer for issues, acting like a subcontractor.

- Asking users to download a free plugin to gain functionality can keep maintenance costs lower for theme developers. It essentially puts the onus on the plugin developer to keep it updated.

- This can actually add functionality to themes without the work. Some plugins add functionality or options as they get updated, so, in a sense, the theme can benefit from this. An example would be a slider that only allowed the use of images, but after an update the slider could show videos as well.

- When a piece of plugin functionality becomes a problem or liability, the theme developer catches a lot less heat for it. After all, it's a plugin managed by another developer or agency, and if all fails there is likely another plugin out there they can start recommending instead.

Cons of using a plugin

- Over time you could end up with a plugin developer taking the functionality in a different direction than you or the theme developer originally anticipated. An example would be a slider that only showed YouTube videos, but after an update it only allows videos hosted on Vimeo.

- Plugin development could stop at any time, leaving you with an old, outdated plugin that you have to find a replacement for. Though the same thing could be said for themes.

Availability of Plugins. At time of this writing there are over 31,890 plugins in the WordPress.org repository, and that's not counting all the plugins distributed directly from developers like Pippin's Plugins, Ben Word and WooThemes. So, I think you will be able to find a suitable replacement for any plugin, should you need to.

- Some plugins that have been embedded may not be properly paid for or licensed. The value of you and/or the developer paying for a plugin goes beyond ensuring you get your questions answered when things go awry. Plugin developers have many of the same bills we do, and by properly buying a plugin (the average $3-30) you are helping to support that plugin developer so they can continue to support you and build new and interesting plugins.

Sidestepping other developers. When a theme developer buys a single license plugin for $3-30 and then embeds it into their theme that sells 25,000 copies (at $30 or even $99 each), you can see where the plugin developer loses out big time. The theme developer should be telling you that a plugin costing $3-30 is recommended/required to add one or more features to the theme. It's the ethical and respectable thing to do for the WordPress community of developers.

On the same note, many plugin developers have a bulk or developer discount for allowing theme developers to bundle a plugin with their themes (often called a "developer's license.") I still believe the plugin should not be embedded into the theme, but instead delivered in the download .zip file with proper licensing attached to let the end user know that a developer license has been paid for and is part of their purchase. This is so much easier than embedding plugins that you would think it the norm of the theme business, but sadly it is not.

Real Talk

WordPress theme developers need to stop hard-coding (embedding) plugins into themes. I know this sounds very black-and-white, and I am sure scores of developers can give me 500 reasons why it's the best thing ever, or tell me about all the customers "demanding" it. But, the truth is that the theme development community at large knows better than to continue this practice of embedding plugins into themes.

I am hoping that this book can also educate the owners and operators of websites that themes packed full of embedded plugin functionality is problematic for all involved. Instead, theme developers should focus on steering users to the appropriate plugins.

Dependency managers like the "TGM Plugin Activation class" (http://tgmpluginactivation.com/) make it incredibly easy to alert Admin users of required or recommended plugins upon activating a WordPress theme.

It's simple, upon activation of the theme, the Admin is alerted that there are required or recommended plugins for the theme, and is shown links to where the plugins are available for download/installation (see image above). The plugins remain independent of the theme, and the onus of maintaining the plugin rests with the plugin developer.

If worrying about plugins being abandoned is what drives developers to add them to the theme, they have a few other options:

- The theme developer can reach out to the original developer to take over the plugin development. Or, they can just fork it and maintain it themselves (as a plugin, of course.)

- There are some developers out there collecting old plugins in the WordPress plugin repository and keeping them going. Alerting these developers to the existence of an abandoned plugin could be a way to get support for a plugin rolling again.

ThemeForest is getting on board. Many people have been pointing the finger at mega-marketplaces like ThemeForest for 'driving' developers towards embedding plugin functionality into themes. It is not a requirement, but one argument is the pressure of getting more sales, getting "elite" status and being on top of their leaderboards. As of today, ThemeForest's theme requirements page state they are looking to take the approach of using plugins over embedding them, and are using the "TGM Plugin Activation class" mentioned above.

Ultimately, theme developers should design themes to look good, and leave the functionality, through utilization of plugins, up to the user. It is a lot easier to give a user a list of suggested plugins that have been tested with the theme than it is to embed it and maintain it in perpetuity. Doing so is actually better for the user/designer in the long term.

Theme Maintenance

Activating and setting up your theme is not the end of the story.

What Does This Mean?

At this stage we are proactively monitoring and maintaining our collection of themes uploaded to our server. This includes the activated theme as well as any installed themes.

Why Do I Have to Do This?

Without maintaining our themes we could end up with broken features, or worse: known security vulnerabilities. On the feature side let's take the case of Twitter upgrading their API where they required a new method of retrieving the latest posts (tweets.) When they did this every theme that had a Twitter feed built into it went dark (broken, empty, no feed, kaput!) This isn't Twitter's fault so much as the fact that the application inside your theme was out of date with the new Twitter API.

If your Twitter feed was being controlled by a plugin, then you would have to only update the plugin, where available. In many cases, the Twitter feed was embedded into the theme meaning the only way to get your Twitter feed working was to get an update to your theme with the new Twitter API.

On the security side, there is a very popular piece of code that goes by the name of TimThumb, and it had a vulnerability in it that hackers exposed and exploited to inject malicious code into websites. Thousands, if not *millions*, of websites were likely compromised, (source: http://blog.sucuri.net/2011/10/timthumb-php-mass-infection-aftermath-part-i.html) displaying links to pharmaceutical and porn sites, and downloading malware to visitors' computers and more.

Above is just one example of a feature and a vulnerability of themes that required attention by theme developers. Over time, virtually every feature, and option of a theme can have issues. It could be something minor, like elements no longer aligning correctly on a page, or something major, like a security vulnerability being discovered. Using an actively supported theme by a knowledgable and proactive developer can ensure you build or own a great, useful website, versus a website that inadvertently sends your users to dodgy pharmaceutical and porn sites or turns your contact form into a spam bot.

What is Involved?

Theme maintenance is fairly simple and threefold. It consists of:

- taking inventory of the themes you have uploaded

- checking for malware, black hat SEO and other problems

- checking for updates and vulnerabilities

Doing inventory

This first one is a recent addition to my maintenance list. I was reading a blog post on Sucuri.net called "Dissecting a WordPress Brute Force Attack" (http://blog.sucuri.net/ 2013/07/dissecting-a-wordpress-brute-force-attack.html) where they witnessed an infected theme being added to their server by an hacker. The theme did not register in the Admin Panel, making it all the more easy to go undetected for months or longer.

It's no longer enough to visit the Themes screen in the Admin Panel to see which themes are installed since we just learned that hackers are now loading bogus and infected themes that don't show up in the Admin. You will need to use the file manager (via your web host's cPanel), or an FTP program to view the contents of your "themes" folder, which is located in the "wp-content" folder.

Inside the "themes" folder you should see an "index.php" file and a folder for each of your themes. If you have two themes installed, there should be two folders, each aptly named so as to correlate to the name of the theme. Note that some developers can get cutesy/funny with the folder names, but it still should be similar to the theme names you are expecting.

You should take note of the theme names installed on your server so you can compare them later. You can write them down in a text file, in a Post marked as private or use a plugin called "Simple Admin Notes" (among others) that adds a tab for you to leave notes for other admins.

As I recommended at the end of chapter 6, you really only need two to three themes installed on your server. With only two, you should know exactly which themes you have installed. For me it's my own custom theme and the latest default WordPress theme (because it's free and gets updated periodically.) If I ever see any additional themes listed in the Themes panel, I know it is spurious and needs to be investigated, and likely deleted.

If you see a folder in the themes folder that you feel shouldn't be there, investigate it by

- seeing if its name matches up with a plugin you have installed. I can't speak for every case, but a plugin developer may have set their plugin to add a folder or file(s) in the themes folder. The W3 Total Cache plugin adds a folder and files to the wp-content folder, so it's not completely out of line for one to add a folder or files to the themes folder (though I have yet to see that happen.)

- using cPanel or FTP to open the folder and view the contents. As we learned in chapter 1B, every theme must come with a style.css file. Does this unknown theme have one? If so, open the file to view the header (first lines of the file beginning with /* and ending with */) to see if there is any useful information or URLs to jog your memory. If there isn't a header, that's a good reason it isn't being recognized by the Admin Panel.

If this is indeed a theme placed by an hacker, renaming it may not keep them out. You must delete the folder and its contents (just be sure not to delete the folder of your active theme!) And, as always, make a backup of your website before you go deleting anything, especially folders.

Scan your site for malware and black hat SEO

Ok, I promise this is easy. So easy you don't even need to log into your Admin or cPanel. Just visit Sucuri.net and enter your website's URL into the area labeled "Scan your website for free." After about a minute, you should see a "SiteCheck Results" page that (hopefully) looks like this:

Sucuri SiteCheck

Free Website Malware Scanner

Anything that is in error, found to be suspect, or a known threat will be listed in red text. This isn't a company that hides the information and makes you pay to see it—it's all very transparent with Sucuri, even going so far as to list the details and actual code of the threat.

If you find your site has been compromised by a hacker, I highly recommend you sign up for one of their plans to get your website cleaned up. I have seen a handful of infected and hacked sites get cleaned up by Sucuri in less than four hours, many of them in two hours. Unless you are a professional, cleaning it up yourself can lead to a very long day and possibly a broken website with lost data. Not only that, you might not clean up the backdoor hackers typically install, so it will just happen again.

> **Pro Tip:** You can scan any website in the world using Sucuri, not just WordPress sites, and not just your own. Meaning, Sucuri is a great tool for scanning websites before you visit them—not every website you visit, but the ones that you feel may be a little suspect. If you are a designer, developer or agency that builds and maintains websites for clients, I highly recommend you take a few moments and have Sucuri scan each of them right now.

The Sucuri Security - SiteCheck Malware Scanner Plugin

Using the Sucuri web app does a good job of scanning your site from the outside. But, I highly recommend using the Sucuri Security - SiteCheck Malware Scanner plugin since it also scans your site from the inside. Why? Because not all files are viewable from the outside. One such case is the uploads and wp-includes folders where it is now common practice from hackers and bots to add PHP files that they can access and execute. Sucuri can scan these as well as alert you to when any WordPress Core files have been changed.

Check for theme updates (via Admin panel)

Keeping your theme up to date is an important security measure, not just a way to get the latest features, options and bug fixes. As we mentioned in the previous chapter, a few years ago a file called TimThumb.php was wildly popular for theme developers (still is.) But, an earlier version had a vulnerability that allowed a hacker to use TimThumb to write a file to your server without having to log in. Since TimThumb was wildly popular in WordPress themes, the vulnerability allowed for thousands of websites to get hacked.

Proactive theme developers either removed the file or updated it with the patched version of TimThumb. But, how do you know they fixed it? How do you know if you have a vulnerability in your theme?

Many themes have the ability to alert you that they need updating, but not all. If you installed a WordPress theme from the WordPress.org repository (typically by using the theme search and upload function in Appearance > Themes > Add New button in your Admin panel), then you will get a notification in your Dashboard > Updates tab like this:

Themes

The following themes have new versions available. Check the ones you want to update and then click "Update Themes".

Please Note: Any customizations you have made to theme files will be lost. Please consider using child themes for modifications.

Update Themes

☐ Select All

☐   **minimalism**
You have version 1.0.1 installed. Update to 1.0.3.

☐ Select All

Update Themes

> **CAUTION:** You must backup your entire website before you update any themes. I'm not even going to mess around with "should", you straight up *must* back up your site. Why? Theme developers can mess up and create bugs you can't live with, theme features can change drastically, or you could have forgotten that you made some custom modification to your theme. **Once you update your theme, the old theme files are overwritten, gone, there is no "undo." Don't risk it: read chapter 5, and have a backup plan/service in place so you can roll back if you need to.**

If you downloaded your theme from a developer's website or a marketplace (other than WordPress.org), you may need to check with their marketing page to see if an update is available. Or you can follow the theme developer on Twitter/Facebook to get alerted to updates. Either way, it's not passive like themes installed directly from WordPress.org, you have to be active about looking for updates, as we will get into now…

Check for theme updates (manual)

If you bought a theme from a marketplace, downloaded it for free from a website or other method, you may need to check for updates manually. To do this, you will need to visit the theme's website/marketing page to see if there is a newer version.

First, go to your Admin Panel and navigate to Appearance > Themes and find the version of the themes you have installed.

If you purchased a theme from a marketplace, it is now time to revisit the marketing page where you bought the theme. If you don't remember where you bought the theme, there are a few ways to figure it out (as mentioned in chapter 8):

- Check your email inbox for a receipt. Most (good) marketplaces will have a link to the marketing page you got the theme from.

- Do a web search for "WordPress theme [enter theme name here]" (without the quotes.) You can find the theme name in your Admin Panel by navigating to Appearance > Themes, and look for the theme labeled "Active." Keep in mind some purchased themes may have the same name as other themes, so double-check the theme page in the search results matches your theme. You can also add the developer's name (hover over theme and click "Details") to your web search to narrow the results. Example: "WordPress Awesome theme by Rad WordPress Themes"

- Look for the stylesheet header in the theme's "style.css" file for a link to theme (or developer) page. A valid theme header will include a "Theme URI" and a "Author URI" (the 'author' is the developer.) You can find this file in your Admin Panel by navigating to Appearance > Editor. The file "style.css" should be the default file shown on the screen. (If for some reason it is not visible, use the "Select theme to edit" pulldown menu on the top right to select your theme.) In some cases, the "Theme URI" link might only point to the main page of the developer, and not the actual theme page as shown below.

 Edit Themes

Specialist: Stylesheet (style.css)

```
/*
Theme Name:    Specialist
Theme URI:     http://templatic.com/cms-themes/specialist-business-wordpress-theme
Description:   Developed by Templatic Team
Version:       1.0.1
Author:        Templatic
Author URI:    http://templatic.com/
*/
```

Compare the version numbers. Most theme developers use a sequence-based numbering system using three levels of updates: major, minor, revision. It typically looks like this: 1.0.1 (for major.minor.revision, respectively.)

This is important to note for a couple reasons;

- One is to help gauge how much of an 'update' you can expect. If your current theme is version 1.0.1, and you see the theme's latest version is 1.9.1, you can see that the developer did nine minor revisions since your version. If the latest theme is 3.0 (technically 3.0.0, but when the revision level is a zero we drop it off to clean it up), you are looking at two major revisions. In all likelihood, this is hardly even the same theme, and some heavy refactoring of the code is likely to have happened. The theme's options panel may look different, as well as a whole new set of features. In fact, any widgets that came with the theme might not work the same way they did before.

- Another reason versions are important is that some developers do not support free updates for major releases. Meaning, if you bought theme version 1.0, you may only get updates until 1.9, but not 2.0 (a major update.) This is not often the case, but this 'lifetime updating' model is in all reality an unsustainable business practice for developers, and some are no longer supporting it.

Oh boy, real talk. Just for fun, or because we all come from different schools of thought, developers do not have a hard-and-fast metric by which to gauge what dictates a major/minor/revision change to the code. What one developer sees as as a minor feature or bug fix to warrant a 'minor' release, another developer might think of as a 'revision.' This major.minor.revision system is meant to be guidelines. It is truly subjective and up to the developer to assign the version numbers.

One theme with a version of 1.5 cannot be compared (on a feature-, bug-, or maturity-level) to a completely different theme that is also on version 1.5. Versioning is only for tracking changes within a theme, not across themes. Themes that are maintained often with progressive features may rise through the versions faster.

Ok, one more. You may come across something that looks like this: "3.6.x" or "3.6+". **These do NOT mean the same thing.** "3.6.x" means 3.6.0 through 3.6.9, but not 3.7. "3.6+" means 3.6.0 on up to the current version (which could be 5.0.) Using "3.6+" in support/marketing documents means they are claiming it is supported beginning with that version.

So, now you found that the developer has a new version for your theme. You will need to download it from them and install it via the Appearance > Themes > Add New > Upload Theme screen in the Admin or via FTP. If you are unfamiliar with a manual install, we'll go over how I prefer to do this below. There are a few different ways, but this one works best for me.

Quick like a bunny! You should read through the following 8 steps before starting and be prepared to do this in quick succession so as to minimize your visitors having to view your site using a different theme. Also, be sure to do this late at night or during off-peak times—also to minimize the amount of visitors having to see the alternate theme.

1) Review your live site and check to make sure it is working as it should before you start working on it. Take screenshots of the pages, if you must. You will need to know that it was working as expected before you started.

2) Download the updated theme to your laptop from the developer or marketplace.

3)   Backup your entire website.

4)   Activate another theme from your list of installed themes: Appearance > Themes.

5)   Using cPanel or FTP, navigate to the "../wp-content/themes" folder and copy the outdated theme's folder to your computer. Once copied over, delete the folder from the server. Do not delete the "../wp-content/themes" folder! That would be bad.

6)   Now upload the updated theme's folder to your server using cPanel or FTP. It's folder should already have the exact same name as the folder you just deleted. If not (which is uncommon and dumb for an update), change it so it does.

7)   Go to Appearance > Themes and activate the uploaded theme. You should now see the updated theme in your Themes screen and live on your site.

8)   Check your site and compare it to step 1 and the theme's marketing page for this version. Is it all working as it should?

What to watch for in a manual update:

- In most cases, your Widgets should remain untouched once you reactivate the updated theme. They will likely be sent to the inactive widgets area (in Appearance > Widgets) during the process, but once WordPress Core sees the theme is back in action, it should reinstate them just as they were. Worse case is that you will have to manually drag them from the inactive widgets area and drop them back into their respective sidebar(s).

- When doing a "dot upgrade" where you go from 3.1.2 to 3.1.5, you should have very little difference in architecture of the theme. It should be a smooth transition with no problems. If you decide to go from 1.0 to 3.0, you may encounter some problems with widgets not automatically going back to their respective sidebars, or sidebars missing altogether. This should be expected when you are performing a serious upgrade.

- In some cases, you may notice that some skins or other customizations made through the theme options screen do not come back. Upon activating the updated theme, you may need to reinstate these options. Another reason you want to do this when fewer visitors are on the site.

- You will need to check the entire site to ensure all your sidebars and widgets and shortcodes are working as they were before. This assumes you knew what your site looked like before, of course.

Manual upgrades using a plugin. You can also use a plugin called "Easy Theme and Plugin Upgrades" to take care of upgrading a theme manually. It saves off the old theme in a .zip file, uploads the new version and boom! you're done. Probably one of the easiest ways to do a 'manual upgrade.' Watch for the same things as listed above. **And always backup your site before you do this.**

Check for theme vulnerabilities

It happens: a developer drops support for a theme, stops working on it, or falls off the map. So, if you want to continue using the theme, you have to maintain the theme yourself. Not everyone is a developer, so what are your options?

Thankfully there are plenty of plugins that can help scan and detect known problems, exploits and vulnerabilities in themes. I won't be able to list them all, so here are a few areas, types or specialties:

- **TimThumb vulnerability checker.** There is a plugin that specifically looks just for the TimThumb code in themes and can update it with a simple click. There are also other vulnerability checkers that scan for the TimThumb code as part of a longer list of known issues. I like plugins that do more than just one thing, so I opt for the latter. As always, backup your entire website before you allow a plugin to make modifications to your code and or database.

- **Anti-virus / anti-malware / malicious code scanners (plugins).** Believe it or not, there are people out there that offer free themes with malicious code embedded in it. And then there are people that inject malicious code via backdoors and other vulnerabilities. Similar to what Sucuri.net does, these scanning plugins are controlled from your Admin Panel, are often automated, and sometimes come with tools that will help you clean up an infection. As always, backup your entire website before you allow a plugin to make modifications to your code and or database.

- **Theme checker.** 'Checking' your theme is a way of comparing the theme's code (PHP and HTML) to the standards set by WordPress.org. A lot has changed over the years, and making sure your theme is using current WordPress best practices is one way of combatting security vulnerabilities, as well as maintaining a fast loading site. There is a great plugin called "Theme-Check," but feel free to use one you like. In the end, you are looking for a plugin that scans all files and folders of a theme and compares it to the set standards by WordPress.org, then gives you a list of recommendations to get your theme 'in spec.' Unless you are a developer, you may want to hire a one to fix your theme. Or, this could be a good time to learn!

You can search for plugins that check for vulnerabilities, malware and perform a theme check by searching the WordPress.org plugin repository in your Admin Panel under Plugins > Add New > Search. Be sure you review the plugin thoroughly before you install it.

> **Use-once plugins.** Some plugins that are a use-once (or even use-infrequently) feature, like Theme-Check, can be deactivated and deleted after you are done with it.

When Should I Do Maintenance?

Let's be frank, WordPress maintenance is boring and tedious stuff, maybe even a bit scary for some. So much so, that many people pay reputable WordPress developers to do this for them (and for some of you that may not be a bad idea.) I actually like monitoring and doing maintenance on my website, but I also know that not everyone has the stomach, patience or confidence for it.

Regardless, every owner/operator of a self-hosted WordPress website should be logging into their Admin Panel about once a week to delete all those spam comments Akismet found (I mean, you are using Akismet or other comment spam filter, right?) and checking plugins for updates (seriously important.) During this time you should notice if there are any theme update notifications, as well as WordPress Core updates.

Let's break it down

- **Weekly** - log in to your Admin Panel and check for plugin updates and delete all spam comments. While this book isn't directly about plugins, keeping your plugins up-to-date is so fundamentally important to the overall security of your WordPress website that I'll say it again: get in the habit of checking and updating your plugins often. In your Admin Panel navigate to Plugins > Installed Plugins and look for notifications of plugins that have updates. If you have updates available, backup your website (see chapter 5) and then update your plugins.

- **Monthly - if you have a theme purchased from a marketplace other than WordPress.org, you might not be enjoying the luxury of your Admin Panel notifying you of an update for that theme.** Some marketplaces/developers are awesome in that they email you when an update is released for a theme you purchased, and tell you what was updated/upgraded. Others may never notify you. You don't have to update every single revision (the third number in a version, as in moving from 1.0.1 to 1.0.2), but at least look for "minor" updates (where it goes from 1.0 to 1.1.)

- **Once every time the theme is updated** - This is really only for themes that are not downloaded via the WordPress.org marketplace. Run the Theme Check plugin to validate the updated theme conforms to WordPress standards (if it doesn't, notify the theme's developer.) Run the virus/malware scan (you never know!) Run the TimThumb vulnerability checker.

> **Pro Tips:** Bookmark the link to your theme's marketing page (where you bought the theme) so you can easily check the version number to see if an update was released. Second best would be to subscribe to their RSS feed, or follow them on Twitter and Facebook where they are likely to also mention theme updates.

What About Multiple Sites?

If you have multiple WordPress websites across different domains, and even across different clients, I recommend looking into a management web app like ManageWP (https://managewp.com/) or Human Made Limited's WP Remote (https://wpremote.com/) to be able to manage all of your WordPress sites from one place. ManageWP even has an app for your phone.

The Pros and Cons of Theme Maintenance

Pros of maintenance

- You will get the latest features and bug fixes, as well as any security patches that were needed.

- You will (hopefully) have a more secure website, thus protecting your visitors.

- You can also benefit from any additional features and options the developer has added.

Cons of maintenance

- The big drawback to doing this is the very real possibility of breaking something. You must understand the state of the theme you are updating before you start.

- If you are currently using a marketplace theme that was customized by another developer, downloading the theme update may overwrite those customizations (depending on how it was customized.) You need to backup the entire website before starting any updates.

> **As a rule:** Don't update any theme that has been customized, unless your intent is to get rid of those customizations. Even then, you should A) save the old theme to your computer, B) contact the developer that customized it in the first place, or C) find a new WordPress theme developer to help you.

The last word on maintenance

- Take control of your themes, know what is on your server, and keep marketplace themes (and plugins!) updated.

- WordPress.org has a set of best practices/requirements/standards for how themes are coded and constructed, and this is found throughout the WordPress Codex: http://codex.wordpress.org/

- The http://codex.wordpress.org/Validating_a_Website page has an extensive list of links that can help you check specific aspects of your theme and its code. Be careful though, for this is developer territory and can lead you down quite a few rabbit holes or end up being way too detailed for some users.

- Some theme marketplaces have their own set of best practices/requirements/ standards for how themes are coded and constructed, and this is found on sections of their website geared toward developer submissions, or by asking them. Note: These can ignore or enforce those dictated by WordPress.org.

- Lastly, always, always, always, always backup your entire website before you do anything to it. There is no reason not to.

Principles of Modifying a Theme

There are two ways to modify a theme: one is my preferred method of using a child theme; the other is to *fork* a theme by altering the original code, thereby making a new theme. **I am not going to go into the actual coding of a theme here, just the concept of modifying a theme.** If you want to learn how to code themes, there are some great books on the subject. Just do a web search for "WordPress theme development," and be sure to read the reviews.

What Do We Mean by Modifying a Theme?

Modifying a theme is different from using the theme's options panel (or plugins) to change fonts, colors, backgrounds and layouts. In the vast majority of cases, when you make changes in the theme's options panel, you are only updating the database. The database holds the information and instructions that reads sort of like this: Theme Awesome font color equals black; Theme Awesome Twitter account equals @tristandenyer; and so on.

In practice, the moment you change any code in the files of a theme it ceases to be that particular theme anymore—it may even look the same visually, but it has been altered. It is now a variant of that original theme. Just as when you paint a white wall green, it ceases to be white. It's still a wall, just as a theme is still a theme, but it is now different.

Today, it is common practice for purchased/marketplace themes to have a custom theme 'options' screen available in your Admin Panel. This is *not* the same as the new WordPress "Customize" functionality found in the Appearance > Customize screen. Both have similar functionality, but themes can have their own separate Admin screen for controlling specific options and features for that theme. This is only available when the theme is activated (see previous chapter on "Activating a theme.")

What is Branching and Forking a Theme?

The only real difference between the two terms is based on your intent. To create a *branch* of a theme is to copy the theme and make updates/changes to the code with the intention of offering it back to the developer as proposed improvements. They would decide to accept (merge) all, some or none or your changes into the original theme as an update to all users of that theme. To *fork* a theme is where you intend to alter the theme's original code with no plans to send your changes back to the theme developer, but instead use the forked theme for your own.

Adding, removing or altering the theme's code can be done in the Admin Panel by navigating to Appearance > Editor, or by editing a local copy of your theme files and overwriting the ones on your server. As you read previously in chapter 6, these are the files that originally came with your theme (or latest theme update.)

Caution: When you alter the original code of a theme it is technically no longer the same theme you downloaded, even if you only make one small change. The theme has now been modified. Modifying the files of a theme (other than the "custom.css" file, explained next) can also void any warranty or support with some developers.

While this may seem obvious, it's important to know when a theme is modified and to track the changes you made so that—should you need to later—you can undo the changes you made. More important, be sure to keep an original copy of a theme, and only modify a duplicate copy of that theme.

Custom CSS: One such case where you may actually modify the theme files by using the theme's options screen is when you add rules to a "custom CSS" box. If available, a custom CSS box is often located in the theme's option screen and is a place where users can add to or override the theme's CSS.

This custom CSS box is often used for modifying how the theme looks, and is reserved for when the theme's options screen doesn't include an option for customization. An example of this would be increasing the space between lines of text in a paragraph (this is "line-height" in CSS, "leading" in printing terms.) Like line-height, there are numerous styling options that are not normally controlled in theme option panels, so the custom CSS box is a catch-all for those that know how to write in CSS.

When you enter CSS rules into the Custom CSS box and save it, you are either A) updating a file in the theme sometimes aptly named "custom.css", or B) updating a field in the database that the theme looks for and adds to each page of the website. (How your theme does this depends on how the developer coded this functionality.) In type A you update the theme files: the custom.css file is loaded after the theme's other CSS files to allow for the custom styles to override the theme styles. In type B you update the database: the theme requests the custom CSS from the database and adds them to the head tag on each page.

At the time of this writing, I highly recommend you use the Simple Custom CSS plugin by John Regan instead of the custom CSS box the theme provides. It's free, very lightweight, won't degrade performance, and keeps all of your custom CSS rules out of the theme's database so you can switch themes later and not lose any of these custom rules (assuming you want them to apply universally.)

What Are Child Themes, and Why Are They Preferred?

I'm going to let these lines from the WordPress Codex explain it better than I could: *"A WordPress child theme is a theme that inherits the functionality of another theme, called the parent theme, and allows you to modify, or add to, the functionality of that parent theme. A child theme is the safest and easiest way to modify an existing theme, whether you want to make a few tiny changes or extensive changes. Instead of modifying the theme*

files directly, you can create a child theme." Source: http://codex.wordpress.org/
Child_Themes

So, let's say the parent theme has the ability to only display a two column layout with the sidebar on the right, but you want the sidebar available on the left for some Pages. You could add that functionality by developing a Child theme that contains a new template for that type of page layout.

Your original theme remains untouched, unchanged; all you are doing is adding a few files in a separate folder of the "wp-content/themes" folder. The style.css file in the Child theme has a line in its header called "Template:" that tells WordPress that it is a Child theme of a specific parent theme:

```
/*
Theme Name: Awesome Child
Theme URI: http://example.com/themes/awesome/
Description: Child theme for our award-winning Awesome Theme
Author: Tristan Denyer
Author URI: http://tristandenyer.com
Template: awesome
*/

@import url("../awesome/style.css");
```

In the example code above, you should see the line "Template: awesome". This tells WordPress to look for a theme folder named "awesome" because that is this child theme's parent. The @import line tells this file to make sure and load the parent theme's stylesheet first, then the child theme's styles.

Things to know about child themes:

- You install, activate, and delete child themes the same way you install, activate, and delete any other theme (see chapters 6, 7 and 13, respectively.)

- On the Appearance > Themes screen, you will see that the child theme becomes the current theme (the active theme), and the parent gets sent down into the list of available themes. A bit of a rant: Why WordPress allows you to delete the parent theme is beyond me. Don't delete the parent since the child theme depends on it.

- The parent theme can get updated without affecting the child theme, but you cannot delete the parent theme. It must remain installed for the child theme to work.

> **Note:** I just noticed that the child themes from Premium Press require you to upload and install them via their theme's options panel (Theme Options > Display Setup > Upload Theme.) They even store their child theme folder inside the parent theme folder. This doesn't make sense to me in that if you update the parent theme the child theme will be discarded or overwritten.
>
> I bring this up because not all themes are created the same, and you may have to work a little differently when it comes to using child theme with premium or custom themes.

- You can have multiple child themes under one parent theme, but you can only have one child active at a time. Also know that you cannot have a single child theme change the functionality of multiple parents. So, one parent, multiple children; but not the other way around.

- In chapter 7 we discovered that when you activate a theme in WordPress it updates the "template" and "stylesheet" records in the wp_options table in your database. The template record in the database will have the name of your parent theme's folder and the "Template:" line in the child theme's style.css. These all need to match, so don't go changing the names of sub-folders in the "wp-content/themes" folder.

- A child theme can be as little as one file—a mandatory file called style.css—or have numerous files and be really complex.

- Knowing that the child theme inherits the functionality of the parent theme and simply adds, removes or modifies that functionality, it needs to have a matching folder structure to its parent. Meaning, if you are looking to modify a file in a folder called "header" that is inside a folder called "templates," your child will need to have these folders in the same order: templates > header > file.

- Some theme developers—such as Studio Press, developers of the "Genesis Framework"—rely heavily on child themes. You may end up needing to buy both a theme and a child theme to get the functionality you need. There are benefits to this in that your parent theme isn't chock-full of every style, option and feature under the sun. You add the style and functionality you need by selecting a child theme. In theory, the parent theme would simply take care of basic, common features and functionality used by all their child themes, leaving the 'heavy lifting' of styling and specific features up to the child theme you choose.

> **Grandchild themes?** For those of you that use frameworks like Genesis and have Child themes, you may want to create a Child to that Child (a Grandchild) to customize it and not lose out on updates. WPSmth.net has an article on how to do this: http://wpsmith.net/2014/wp/theme-framework-child-themes-grandchild-themes/

When Should I Modify a Theme?

There are a few main reasons people modify themes, or add child themes:

- to fix a bug or layout problem

- to add/modify functionality

- add another layout option

- or clone the theme to use it as a starting point for another custom theme (known as "forking", mentioned above.)

Theme's got bugs, and no support

If you are using a theme that is no longer supported (the developer stated there will be no further updates), then modifying the theme is usually the best way to fix bugs and layout issues. I still, and always, recommend you keep an original copy of the theme to revert back to should things go wrong. In many cases, bug fixes will require modifying the original file(s) of the theme, not uploading a whole new child theme.

Need to add some functionality

This is where I stop everyone and make them answer a couple questions: 1) what do you want to add?, 2) could you do this with a Child theme, or is there a plugin for that? Your best course of action is to do a web search for "WordPress plugin [then describe the functionality]" (without quotes.) Examples: "WordPress plugin for latest twitter posts", or "WordPress plugin event calendar", or "WordPress plugin custom sidebars."

You will be amazed at the number of plugins that are available for WordPress. But, as with everything, you should exercise caution. Needing (or wanting) 15 pieces of functionality and finding 15 plugins to take care of it may not be a wise move either. At that point, you may want to see if one premium plugin can handle multiple needs, or if switching to another more capable theme might not be a better choice.

> **Premium plugins** are similar to "premium" themes in that they are sold by developers or marketplaces, often come with good-to-great documentation and tutorials, as well as support. Plugins you get for free may have documentation and some support (even great support), but they are often a use-at-your-own-risk type product. But, don't let the act of paying for a plugin sway you, for I have downloaded some amazing and fully functional free plugins while I have also paid for some janky and worthless plugins. In fact, about 98% of the plugins I use today are free to use.

Need more layout options

There may be times when you find your theme does not give you the flexibility you need for certain content. Some themes do not come with a full-width layout (no sidebars), or the ability to swap the sidebar to the other side. Controlling and styling the layout is the core responsibility of a theme, so this is a great example of when you may want to modify your theme to suit your needs by developing a Child theme.

Want to fork the theme

Some developers use existing themes as a starting point for creating their own themes. They clone the theme files and then make modifications to them until the theme looks and acts the way they want. Or, in some cases, they take parts from a few themes and use them to create a new theme. While the end result originated from another theme (or three), it is essentially now a unique theme.

But, there are a few gray areas to doing this. You want to keep in mind that another developer wrote all or most of that code, and a designer may have spent hours working on the look and feel, as well as all the background images available. To open up a theme and see how they pull in recent Posts to the homepage is one thing, but to grab all the background images they are offering and add that to your theme is not ethical. You should take the time to design your own background images and make your theme look unique.

> **The license.** All WordPress themes are GNU General Public License (GPL), meaning that all end users can use, share, modify, copy the theme, even if they bought it or hired a developer to code it. As far as themes go, I think WordPress.org puts it best: *"Contrary to popular belief, GPL doesn't say that everything must be zero-cost, just that when you receive the software or theme that it not restrict your freedoms in how you use it."* To 'Use a theme' also includes modifying or copying the entire theme or parts thereof. Ethics are what keeps one from copying a theme another developer wrote, making no modifications, and selling it as their own creation. That, and a community of developers who will publicly shame you into seeing the light. (Quote source: http://wordpress.org/themes/commercial/)

The Pros and Cons of Modifying a Theme

Pros of modifying

The best part about modifying a theme is getting under the hood and seeing how it all works. Then making little tweaks and additions to end up with a theme you had a hand in developing. There is something fun and exciting about that. And there is also something to be said for making something better (hopefully), or more importantly, making it work better for your particular need.

It's kind of like upgrading a gas water heater in your house: it requires technical skills and tools, is a little dangerous, and if done wrong can leave the house without hot water (or with a gas leak.) But, when when you're done and everything works, you remember that afternoon every time the hot water comes out of the faucet. And that can be an awesome feeling.

In virtually all cases, you should only modify a theme when you have no expectation of ever installing an updated version of that theme. Once you modify the theme files, the next time you go to update the theme it is very likely (more like a certainty) that the modifications you made will be overwritten with the update's files. Knowing what you updated and attempting to go in to each update to remake those changes is not only tedious, it may be incredibly complicated. Some themes make drastic changes to their layout and functionality, and depending on what you modified, the changes may not work as before.

Cons of modifying

Since you really should be using a Child theme to modify any theme you intend to update in the future, there isn't much I could say that should discourage you from modifying a theme. I could go out on a limb and say that modifications made by an inexperienced developer may be unstable or break the layout of your site. But, again, if you did it using a child theme you could simply turn it off by re-activating the Parent theme.

Preserve Your Work

As I outlined above, once you modify theme files it can no longer be updated without losing the modifications you made. Ensure your work is preserved by keeping good notes which track the changes you made, by effectively warning those who may come after you that they risk losing functionality if they update, or by turning off update notifications altogether.

How To Keep Good Notes

A good, thoughtful developer will help out other developers (and themselves) by leaving comments in their code. It's like Post-It notes, or helpful tips meant for those that have to work on the code after them (and to remind themselves of what they did.)

If you make any changes to a theme, it's a good idea for you to leave a similar comment or note in the theme that shows in the Appearance > Themes > Details screen to alert admins that this theme should never be updated, or that if they do so, it is with the understanding it may overwrite any changes that were made.

You can do this via the Appearance > Editor tab. Here's how:

1)   Navigate to the Appearance > Editor tab. You should see the "style.css" file open in the editor. Make sure the theme you want to add a note to is listed as being selected in the top right drop down menu. In the editor look for the "Description" line at the top of the "style.css" contents. This is the stylesheet header that populates the information in the Themes tab. You can rewrite the text that is in the "Description" line, just make sure you do not delete the "Description:" part, or any other line prefix for that matter.

2)   Enter a new line of text wrapped in a strong tag like this to make it bold:
     `<strong>Do NOT update this theme! The codebase has been customized and updating it will overwrite those customizations.</strong>`

3)   Click "Update File" button, and navigate to the Appearance > Themes tab to

see your work in action.

What is notable about this sort of comment/note is that it can only be viewed by visiting the Appearance > Themes > Details screen. Anyone updating themes via the Dashboard will not see this note.

> **Go figure..there's a plugin for notes.** Someone actually made a plugin called "Simple Admin Notes" (among others) that adds a tab for you to leave notes for other admins. I'd recommend using that for not only what we did above, but for other important information about your website (but not passwords…that is a seriously bad idea.)

How To Block Theme Update Notifications Altogether

Leaving notes for yourself and other admins can be tedious and leaves room for error. Unless you want to be the only admin so other users with lesser roles can't update themes, the other option to keep people from updating themes is to block the theme update notification. I do not recommend doing this since it blocks update notifications for all of your themes, but if you have to, there is a plugin called "Disable WordPress Theme Updates" by John Blackbourn.

What Happens When We Switch a Theme?

According to WordPress.com's stats, we can see that well over a million users of their web app switch themes each month: http://en.wordpress.com/stats/misc/ This is not even taking into account the self-hosted WordPress users that also switch, so that number is likely a lot higher.

The act of switching a theme is one of the easiest things you can do in WordPress, and WordPress.com claims "switching your theme is instant and requires no rebuilding." (Source: http://wordpress.com/stats/misc/) While that may be true for some users, switching themes presents risks that must be understood in order to prevent losing important content and/or functionality.

How Do I Switch a Theme?

It's easy:

WordPress version 3.7 and below: in the Admin Panel you navigate to Appearance > Themes and select "Activate" on one of the themes under "Available Themes."

WordPress version 3.8 and 3.9 (current version at time of writing): in the Admin Panel you navigate to Appearance > Themes, hover over the theme you want and select "Details," then "Activate.

Then you spend the rest of the weekend wondering why things are missing from your website, or moved, or not presenting correctly. It happens, and it really bums me out to know that themes are sold as being this easily interchangeable thing—"Make your website look like new with Awesome Theme!", "Upgrade your website with a new theme for only $30!", or "Fast and easy setup".

I'm not here to bum you out, but if you have an existing website using multiple shortcodes across Pages and Posts, with images and widgets in the sidebar, switching a theme is rarely ever a 10-minute project. If your website is huge and complex with a lot of widgets, the reality is it could take you a couple hours or a couple days to get it all switched over.

Think back to the house analogy I used in chapter 1A. We can extend that analogy and say the bigger your house and the more stuff you own the longer it takes to remodel. The same typically goes for websites.

But, that being said, I can promise you that planning ahead can make the switch to a new theme very straightforward and happen much faster and with fewer complications.

What is Going to Happen?

Once you activate another theme, all of the styling and functionality of the previous theme will no longer show to your visitors. Some of your content will show, but anything that was being populated or controlled by the previous theme will not show. There are numerous types of content a WordPress website can control, populate and display to visitors, so I will only cover the most common ones here.

Blog Posts

The contents of blog posts (HTML, text and links to images) are stored in your database, so no matter what theme is active, the HTML, text and images you entered into your Posts will continue to show to your visitors. The new theme simply styles them in a different way.

> **WTF.** Depending on the theme, the developer may not have styled the blog roll or the blog posts. Strange, I know, but I occasionally come across a theme like this where it wasn't intended to be used as a blog. Check the theme's marketing pages or instructions for details.

If you were displaying recent or sticky Posts to your homepage, they might not work the same way in the new theme. Whether or not a theme allows sticky posts is up to the theme developer, so not all themes have this functionality. Just because they are not showing on the homepage does not mean they were deleted. Activating a different theme does not delete blog posts.

Custom Post Types

It is becoming increasingly popular for themes to come with their own custom post types. By default every WordPress site uses post types to declare some content you create as a Page, or a Post, or an Attachment. But now developers can add custom posts to their themes that the user can assign to their content. I have seen "video," "photoblog," "gallery options" and more being used.

The problem is that when you go to switch your theme, your database will continue to link your content with whatever custom post type you originally chose, but your new theme won't know what to do with it. Custom post types are part of the theme files, and in this case your new theme may not be looking for the same post type as your previous theme.

If your previous theme used "photoblog" as a custom post type and your new theme also uses the exact same name for their custom post type, then you could see the new theme add its styling to all content assigned to the "photoblog" custom post type. Conversely, if your previous theme used "photoblog" as a custom post type and your new theme doesn't have that custom post type, it will likely use the default "Post/Page" post type.

Basically, your database is telling your new theme "Hey, this piece of content is a photoblog post type!" But, your new theme doesn't have a "photoblog" custom post type, so it says "I don't know what you are talking about, so I'm going to ignore this 'photoblog' mumbo-jumbo and show it as a regular 'post.'" Your content is still there, but the styling and functionality you once had for posts labeled "photoblog" (whatever it was) is gone. Until you go in to edit the Post and choose a new custom post type, it will always be listed as a "photoblog" custom post type in your database. Which will be a good thing in the event you decide to switch back to the previous theme.

Pages

Like blog posts, the contents of Pages are stored in your database, so no matter what theme is active, the copy and images you entered into your Pages will continue to show to your visitors. The new theme simply styles them in a different way.

Where it gets tricky is if the theme used Custom Fields to populate parts of any page. Custom Fields are used for allowing the author of a Page or Post (or other custom post type) to add metadata to the page. An example would be a text area on a list of products that contained a short description of each product. The user would add this to each individual product page in the Custom Fields section.

The problem arises when you switch themes because the new theme likely does not have the same Custom Field name. It won't know what to do with the content in the Custom Field and will likely ignore it. You may find yourself going into each Page and having to update the Custom Field drop down in order to use the new name established by the new theme.

Sliders (slideshows)

This is going to hurt on a couple different levels. One is that the vast majority of themes use slider plugins that are embedded into the theme. The settings will stay with the old theme, while any images you uploaded specifically for the slider should remain in the Media Library and be usable by the new theme. The problem is that you may need to create new images for the new slider since it will likely be a different size.

Some sliders are auto*magic*ally populated by using the featured images from recent Posts and Pages. In some cases this can be a much easier transition. Otherwise, you may have to manually populate each slide of the new slideshow.

If you love populating your Pages and Posts with sliders or image galleries, then I highly recommend using a slider plugin instead of any slider option the theme offers. This way, when you switch themes the sliders go with you and the settings are honored.

Drag & Drop page builders

One of the hardest things I have had clients deal with is the fact that when they customize the layout of a Page or Post using some nuclear-powered, proprietary drag & drop page builder, it will never look that way after they switch themes. In fact, I have seen some homepages turn into soup sandwiches because the old theme allowed the owner to move around elements of the page using a drag & drop page builder, and the new theme relied on widgets to populate the sections. These two means of displaying and arranging content are not interchangeable.

Ok, horror story time! I had a client with an existing theme that used a drag & drop page builder for every page on her site. She had it all dialed in just the way she wanted it with columns and grid layouts. She also diligently updated her WordPress Core. Then one day the page builder would not allow her to update any of the content inside the drag & drop modules. I reverted the WordPress Core back to a previous version and it worked, so something was in conflict between the theme and WordPress.

She figured it was time to move on to a new theme anyway. When she made the switch, she found that all of the Page and Post content was mashed up into one long paragraph, each section in a random order. It was technically still in the database, but the new theme didn't recognize how the theme was storing the content in the database, so it simply dumped it all into the page editor's WYSIWYG. We reverted back to the old theme, copied all the content to text doc, switched the theme, added the text back in and never looked back.

Not all drag & drop page builders are bad (though I could not in good conscience ever recommend you use a theme that relies heavily on it.) Just keep in mind that the more tricked out and complicated the page builder, the more problems you may run into when you switch over to a different theme.

I recommend that if you like drag and drop editors, use one that is a plugin and not part of the theme. This way when you switch themes, all your dragging and dropping will be honored in the new theme's Page and Post content areas.

Images, PDFs, and other Media Library contents

Let's start with images first, since they are the trickiest and often the most ill-treated contents in WordPress sites. When you upload an image to your WordPress site using the 'add new media' functionality, your theme tells your WordPress Core to resize the images into specific sizes and save them. You can view these sizes in the Admin Panel under Settings > Media. Know that the original image you uploaded will be saved, but then (in virtually all cases) three other sizes of that image will be created and saved as well, for a total of four images for every upload.

These images do not change size once uploaded. So, if your new theme's blog roll is asking for a "thumbnail" sized image to populate a spot that is 170 pixels wide, but all of your current "thumbnail" images are 150 pixels wide, you may be left with some extra blank space around the image. This is especially true when a theme developer overrides common image sizes to accommodate some special design they have going on. Once you switch themes, that custom/odd image size may become practically useless in your new theme. If you uploaded a bunch of images, that could account for a lot of image assets that will just collect dust.

PDFs, Word documents, Excel spreadsheets can also be uploaded to your Media Library. Since these are not images, WordPress will simply store them in your "uploads" folder and not convert or compress them. If you are linking to a document from a Page or Post, all themes will honor that link since that is basic HTML functionality not dictated by the theme. How they choose to display the document after a user clicks on the link is a whole different matter. Some themes may be set up to display documents inline with the contents of the Page/Post, others may open it in a lightbox (a form of popup window.)

Social media

It is very common for today's themes to come with a Twitter feed designed into the theme itself so it can be controlled in the theme's option panel. This is different than you adding a Twitter widget plugin because the code is actually part of the theme, whereas a plugin can be removed. With an embedded feature like a Twitter feed, you will not be taking that with you when you switch to a new theme. Even if the new theme has a Twitter feed capability, you will need to set it up again with that particular theme. Same goes for any other social media integration the theme may offer.

Many themes also come with share buttons on Pages and Posts that are part of its set of features. Your new theme will likely have them too. If not, and you want to keep them, you will need to find a "social sharing" plugin to add these back into your new theme. Though, if you read chapter 2, you will know I recommend you not use social sharing buttons on your site.

Widgets

Lots of people love to be able to customize their sidebars to their liking, and we rely heavily on widgets to do much of the work. It is important to know that there is a big difference between the widgets that come with the WordPress Core installation, and those that come with the theme (and there are some that come from plugins.)

Every widget supplied by the theme will not be there when you switch to a new theme. Even if the new theme also has a similarly named widget, the old widget is part of the old theme. It is possible for the themes to use the exact same code for the widget (if made by the same developer), but even then the content and settings of the widget may not carry over to the new theme, or it may be listed in the "Inactive Widgets" area of the Widgets screen.

Inactive Sidebar (not used)	▾
This sidebar is no longer available and does not show anywhere on your site. Remove each of the widgets below to fully remove this inactive sidebar.

| Text: More posts ▾ | Custom Menu ▾ |

Inactive Widgets	▾
Drag widgets here to remove them from the sidebar but keep their settings.

| Pages: Pages ▾ |

Screen capture showing the Inactive Sidebar and Inactive Widgets sections.

A (possible) way around this: I ran couple tests to see what happens when the widgetized areas are coded the exact same way across a few themes. I found that by using the same code that creates widgetized areas across all functions.php and sidebar.php files, you can essentially keep your widgets in place when switching between themes. I've tried this across only three themes, so I won't exactly call it bulletproof.

If you are asking a developer to custom build a new theme for you and would like to retain the widgets in their respective widgetized areas, ask to see if they could copy them from the theme files you have now. Though, if you only have a couple widgets to move back in place, this can be more hassle than the 5 seconds it would take to drag them a few inches across the screen.

Developers: this may be a great idea to allow your users to switch between your themes and save them one extra step. Though, it would require some foresight and planning.

Fonts, colors, backgrounds...

If you selected special fonts, font sizes, colors and backgrounds in the theme options screen, they too will not carry over to the new theme, and will need to be set up again. It is important to note that not all themes have the same choices, so you may need to settle on a new font, size or background image after you switch to the new theme.

What About Parent and Child Theme Setups?

For those of you that have a Child theme installed and activated, you must understand that you cannot delete the Parent theme. The Child theme is dependent on the Parent. Deleting the Parent theme will cause the Child theme to not work and it will be moved to the "Broken Themes" section of the Themes screen.

Screen capture of the the Broken Themes section at the bottom of the Themes screen.

Parents in the basement, Children upstairs

When you are using a Child theme WordPress will deactivate the Parent theme and show it in the Themes screen as an installed theme. This is a bit confusing for some in that there is no visual relationship or obvious dependancy. You have to rely on a small line of text in the active theme details. Can you find it in the image below?

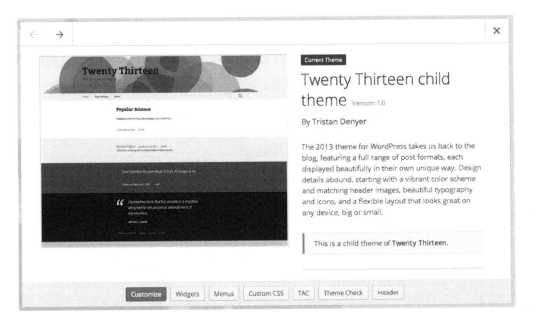

Screen capture showing a Child theme as an "Active Theme."

WordPress will not stop you from deleting a Parent theme that has an active Child depending on it being installed. And there is no visual indication on the Parent theme that it has a Child depending on it. If you delete the Parent theme, WordPress will revert to the default theme, and will consider the Child theme "broken."

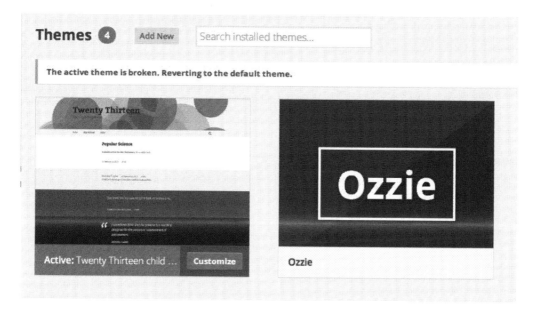

Screen capture of the Themes screen showing alert message that the active theme is broken because I deleted its Parent theme. Refreshing this page will show the default theme (Twenty Fourteen) as active.

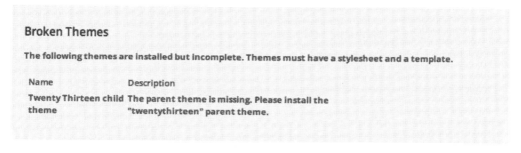

Screen capture showing the "Broken Themes" section at the bottom of the Appearance > Themes screen. This happened because I deleted its Parent theme.

> **Pro Tip:** Always leave the default theme installed as your fallback theme. The reason for this is that WordPress will automatically activate it if your active theme gets deleted, goes missing or is considered "broken" because of missing files.
>
> If you are missing the default theme, it will still try and load it as a placeholder, and your visitors will see a blank white page, or an error.
>
> WordPress 3.6 and 3.7 use the "Twenty Thirteen" as its default theme, 3.8 and 3.9 use "Twenty Fourteen."

Switching while using a Child theme

Parent-to-Child. When you switch to a new Parent theme while using a Child theme the new Parent theme is the only theme that WordPress cares about. The previous Child theme is deactivated and stored in the Appearance > Themes screen with any other inactive themes you have installed.

Child-to-Child. If you are actively using a Child theme, and are looking to switch to another Child theme, you can do so directly. Meaning you simply activate the new Child theme; no need to activate the Parent theme first (though, the Parent needs to be installed on your server prior to activation.)

Straight to Child. If you are planning on installing new Parent and Child themes, you can install both and simply activate the Child. Unless your theme developer expressly instructed you to do so, there is no need to activate the Parent before the Child. The Child will simply look for the Parent theme to be installed.

So, How Do I Plan?

There are numerous moving parts to a website. Seriously, there are a bazillion details, options and features available in almost a bazillion themes in the world, so I won't be able to cover each in detail. I am going to show you what to look for and how to plan for most sites. You may find your situation requires a bit more tweaking, but the idea of planning is the same nonetheless.

Before we do so, you have to ask yourself:

- **Are you looking to preserve as much of the look and feel and placement of**

sidebar items as possible? If so, I'm not going to kid you: you are looking at a long road ahead of you that requires a detailed inventory and plan.

- **Or are you simply concerned with content and don't mind moving things around during setup?** This is much easier to deal with, and, let's be frank, a more rational approach to managing a website. It's a website, things are meant to change over time! (And frankly, Google likes when websites get updated since it shows signs of life.)

Using what we learned above, we will get in deep with the theme's options screen (if it has one), the Admin Panel, the widgets screen, plugins screen, and Pages and Posts. This is where we will find what is inherent to the theme.

I recommend you take notes and copy what you want to transfer over to the new theme in a text document. Do not use a Word document since copy and pasting from them into WordPress can be problematic in that formatting from Word can be pasted into WordPress.

For those of you on WordPress 3.9 and use the Visual Editor, there is now a "Paste as Text" button available in the WYSIWYG Toolbar section. This removes the formatting that is in Word. Mac users can still use `cmd-opt-shift-v` to paste without formatting.

Theme Options screen

Look for the theme's options panel in the left nav bar. It can be located in the top-level of the nav as a new custom looking tab, or under the Appearance tab typically listed as "[theme name] options" (see example below.) If your theme does not have its own options panel, then skip this section.

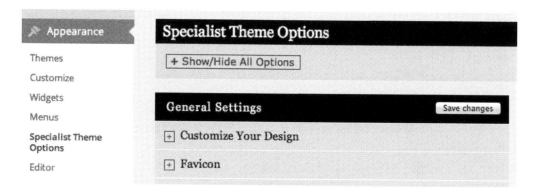

Screen capture of the Theme Options screen in the Specialist theme from Templatic.

Depending on how closely you are trying to mimic the old theme's styling, you will need to start taking inventory of things like fonts, colors, location of your logo image file. Some theme option panels even control the copyright text found in the footer, as well as custom CSS.

> **Custom CSS.** Do not copy over the contents of the custom CSS box unless you are sure it is specific to formatting and styling for special or universal content in a Page or Post. In most cases, you do not need this, but you can preserve it in your text doc if you feel you may need it.
>
> For styling of special or universal content that is not part of the theme I recommend using the Simple Custom CSS plugin by John Regan. This way, when you switch themes the custom CSS rules you wrote remain in place.

Once you have copied all the of the settings from your Theme Options screen, we can move on to the widgets.

Widgets screen

Navigate to the Appearance > Widgets screen. Here we will take stock of the widgets that are being used—this is the column on the right of the screen capture below:

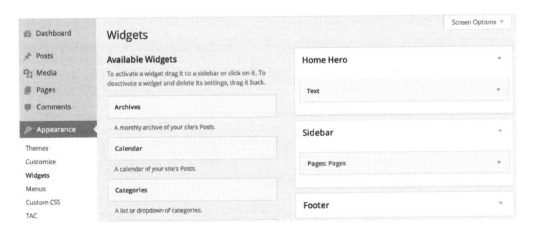

Screen capture of the Widgets Screen showing three widget areas on the right.

In the image above, you can see that the top two widget areas (on the right) are expanded to show one widget each. The footer is currently shown in its collapsed state.

For collapsed widget areas, click on the down arrow to expand the widget area and view the widgets assigned to them.

As stated earlier in this chapter, not all themes have the same widgets areas, let alone the same number of areas. The theme shown above has three areas, while some themes may have none, one, or even a dozen or more.

What you want to do here is take note of what widgets are in what widgetized areas. In the above image, I would expand the "Text" widget in "Home Hero" and take note of its contents and that it was assigned to the "Home Hero" widget area. This will all be worth it when you have to assign these to the new widget areas in the new theme—you do this by dragging them from the "Inactive Widgets" area at the bottom of this screen to the new widget areas.

If you ever see a widget that has your theme's name in the title of it, you can bet it is a part of the theme—you won't see that widget when you switch to the new theme. Meaning: say my current theme is called Awesome Theme and it has a widget called "Awesome Theme Twitter." I know that widget will no longer show—and will not be in the "Inactive Widgets" section—when the new theme called Rad Theme is activated.

Plugins screen

Navigate to the Plugins screen. This part is where you are looking for theme-specific plugins: ones that are installed to support the theme you are currently using, but may not use in the new theme. These can be a Twitter feed, an Instagram gallery, a homepage slider, etc.

In the earlier chapters we talked about how not all themes can do all the things, so a plugin may be necessary. Your new theme may have some functionality that is more robust than the plugin that performs a similar function. You will want to take note of any settings (such as a Twitter/Instagram handles) so you can set up the new theme's functionality quickly without having to hunt for it.

And yes, I did say earlier that I prefer my functionality to be handled by a plugin and not the theme. I know the above statement seems counter to that, but the reality is that the vast majority of readers will not follow my advice and will choose to use the theme functionality over any plugin they may have in place.

Also, there is a very real possibility that your new theme requires you to use its embedded Twitter feed or slider functionality in order to populate areas of the homepage. I have seen this scenario in quite a few themes where some widget-like areas are handled in the Theme Options screen instead of the Widgets screen or a plugin.

Lastly, there is no easy 1-2-3 instruction on how to find theme-specific plugins. This will require you doing some Sherlock Holmes-like investigative work on the plugins you have activated and comparing their functionality to what is claimed on the new theme's marketing page. Example: if you see a plugin called "Full screen backgrounds", and you know your new theme has full screen background slider functionality, it is a good bet that you won't be using that plugin anymore. Or maybe you will? These are things you will have to work out on your own before you make the switch.

Pages and Posts

Since Pages and Posts typically take up the bulk of a website's content this part can be a tedious, though necessary step of this process.

What we are doing is mainly looking for shortcodes (I discussed shortcodes in chapters 1B, 7, 8, and elsewhere in this book.) Though, you may encounter problems with drag & drop editors and other theme-specific functionality that was added to Pages and Posts. Since shortcodes are the most common, I'll cover them here.

Unless you know you have a plugin that is adding shortcodes to your Pages/Posts, you can typically assume all shortcodes are processed by the theme and or inherent WordPress shortcode functionality. This means that they will very likely not work in the new theme, and simply display to your visitors in their raw form like this: `[shortcode_name]`.

I recommend installing a plugin such as the new "Orbisius Broken Shortcode Checker" (on CodeCanyon) to do a search for any shortcodes that are "broken" by the new theme so you don't have to go through all the Pages/Posts by hand. If you have an unholy ton of shortcodes that are broken, you can use the "Hide Broken Shortcodes" plugin to—you guessed it—hide them so your visitors don't see them in their unprocessed state. This buys you some time so you can elect to clean them up later.

As for drag & drop editors and other theme-specific functionality, I have found they are not as common as shortcodes and simply offer too many variables for me to adequately cover here. Take a few mins to open a good sample of your Pages and Posts in the Admin Panel and look for anything that stands out as being other than regular text or images. Note the Page/Post URL so that when you switch your theme you can quickly investigate that Page/Post for issues.

When Should I Switch a Theme?

For those of you using a development or staging site, this section does not apply to you. It's really for those readers that are planning on doing this on a live, production site. While it is highly recommended to make major upgrades and changes on a development site then migrate it over to production, the reality is that the vast majority of people will switch out their theme on a live site.

Time needed to make the switch

If you have a website with little to no traffic you can switch a theme anytime since no one is really going to see it. But, if you have a site that has a good amount of traffic, I recommend getting the research and planing mentioned above done first and setting aside a good block of time before you make the switch. You will want to do the bulk, or all, of the switch-over in one fell swoop.

If you have a website with little to no Posts, Pages, widgets, and shortcodes, then you can switch a theme rather quickly since it may not take very long at all. Sites with a ton of Posts, Pages, widgets, and shortcodes, I recommend getting your plan together and setting aside a good block of time before you make the switch.

I also highly recommend you switch your theme when you have a block of a few hours to put things back in place, make necessary fixes, take care of any surprises, and test it. You may not need a few hours, but if you only give yourself 30 minutes to perform a switch, you may run out of time and have to switch back, or have your visitors see your site with some missing features for the time being.

Why Should I Switch a Theme?

What we haven't covered yet is the reasoning behind wanting or needing to switch a theme. While the reasons can be numerous and varied, I'll cover a few good reasons one may want or need to switch themes. Each are also assuming that you don't have development knowledge to fix it yourself.

No more support

If you are running an older theme that the developer has dropped support for, you may want to switch to a newer theme that has support. While I am still using a theme on a site that was built over 5 years ago and no longer has support, I could not recommend you to do the same.

Technology changes so fast. What was rock solid for WordPress 2.7 in 2009 may not be so solid today. At that time Google's browser Chrome was just released and hardly used, and many were still using Internet Explorer 7! Today's themes are built for and tested on a different set of benchmarks for browser technology, and phones, and screen sizes that didn't exist 5 years ago.

Missing/outdated technology

Your theme may be recent and still be supported by a developer, but doesn't have the technology or functionality you require from it today. Examples could be that your theme is not responsive and doesn't show well on mobile devices. Making a theme responsive is not as easy as adding a plugin, so making the switch to a responsive site may be far less expensive than asking a developer to rework the HTML, CSS and JavaScript.

An outdated technology example could be an old Twitter feed that no longer works (we discussed this issue in chapter 10.) An outdated Twitter feed should not be the only reason you make the switch, since you can often add a Twitter plugin or update the theme. But, when it starts to add up where you have two or more parts of the site no longer working, you will want to start looking for a new theme.

Plugin conflicts

When you add plugins to your site and start to notice many of them come up with errors after being activated, you may have either A) chosen a lot of badly coded plugins, or B) are having a conflict with your badly coded theme. Some plugins will be generous and tell you what the problem is so you (or your developer) can fix it. In far worse cases it takes down the whole website and leaves you with a blank white page displaying only a PHP error.

If this happens once out of dozens of plugins you have used, then I would investigate the plugin. If you install three plugins and an error or problem arises for each, then I would start investigating the theme (though you could find that you picked three badly coded plugins, too.)

Recently developed/updated themes that are following good WordPress coding practices should not have issues with plugins that are following good WordPress coding practices. Just another reason to stick to quality themes and plugins that have great support from attentive developers.

Design and layout problems

As we talked about in previous chapters, you can use a Child theme to help add or remove page elements, features, and functionality. But someone has to code that Child theme. If you don't know how, you will need to pay a developer to do so.

If you only need a small or minor change to the design and layout, then a Child theme may be worth it by not having to go through the hassle of finding a new theme and switching it out. A small or minor change/upgrade could include setting up a full-width page (no sidebar), adding support for a sidebar on the opposite side of the page, adding a widget area, or redesigning the layout of the footer.

Changes to the font size, colors, background colors, line height of text, and things of the like can be done using the Simple Custom CSS plugin by John Regan, no Child theme would be needed.

Major changes such as making the site responsive, converting it from HTML 4 to HTML5, or major structural changes to the layout would require so much work that getting a new theme will be much more cost effective (and less troublesome.)

What Does Deactivating Mean?

Switching a theme means you are essentially deactivating one and activating the other. And as I mentioned right from the beginning, you can have only one theme active at a time. Even in the event of using a Child theme, the Child theme is activated and the Parent is not active (the Parent just needs to remain installed so the Child can reference it, so DO NOT delete it in part or in whole.)

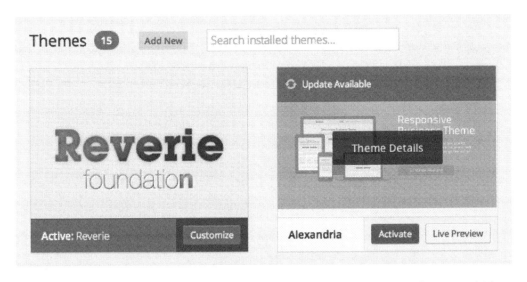

The screen capture above shows two themes in the Themes screen (WordPress 3.8.) The one on the left is the active theme, and the one on the right is the installed theme (not active.)

Technically, "deactivating" a theme is not actually a function you can perform. The action WordPress allows you to do is to "activate" a theme. When you click on "activate" on a theme listed in Appearance > Themes > Details, you are telling WordPress to replace the current theme in use with that one, which then automatically deactivates the current live theme.

A deactivated theme is not the same as a deleted theme. The deactivated theme will remain on your server in the "../wp-content/themes/" folder until you delete it (see next chapter.)

One more thing to note: there is no mention or listing of "deactivated" themes in WordPress. There are only installed themes (chapter 6) and active themes (chapter 7.) An installed theme is the same thing as a deactivated theme.

What Happens During Deactivation?

As we learned in chapter 7, activating a theme tells WordPress to update the "template" and "stylesheet" records in the wp_options table in your database to use the new theme. Since you must activate a new theme in order to deactivate the current theme in use, your database is essentially changing the theme name in the wp_options table.

The settings and content associated with the old theme are stored in the database should you ever need to re-activate the old theme. This is how you can reactivate a theme you once used and find your theme options, custom fields and widgets all repopulated.

On that note, what doesn't happen during deactivation is any cleaning up of information in the database. If you are on your 4th theme, all the settings data associated with all four themes is still in the database. If you were to reactivate one of those old themes, you would see the original settings come back to life.

Think about it: each time you activate and use a theme you are storing a lot of data about that theme in the database. Do that 4, 5 or twelve times and you could have one bloated database full of information you may never use again.

Cleaning up your database. This is a bit out of scope for this book, but since I mentioned it above you may want to look into cleaning up your database of old information. I recommend doing a web search for "cleaning up WordPress database" to find a lot of helpful articles and plugins on the subject. And, as always, make sure you backup your website before you 'clean' your database.

Uninstalling/Deleting A Theme

There may come a time that you want to completely remove a theme from your server. I'll go so far as to guess that the vast majority of self-hosted WordPress installations have at least one theme too many installed. Maybe even dozens. Repeating myself from earlier: you only need the theme you are using (and its Parent, if you are using a Child theme), and one backup theme. So, two to three themes at most.

What Happens When I Uninstall/Delete a Theme?

The choice of action words by WordPress is a bit odd in that you "install" a theme, but there is no "uninstall", only "delete." Uninstall and delete mean virtually the same thing to WordPress. In chapter 6 we learned that installing a theme is simply storing it in the "themes" folder on your server. It needs to be activated before the world can see it and you can start using it. Therefore, uninstalling a theme means you are removing it from the themes folder on your server by deleting it.

> **Caution:** Do not delete the folder or files of an active theme. There's a reason WordPress does not offer "delete" in the Admin Panel for the active theme, only inactive ones: you need to always have one theme activated. So, in WordPress we activate a new theme in order to swap out themes, never leaving the website without styling (as we went over in chapter 12.)

How Do I Delete My Theme(s)?

WordPress makes it pretty easy to delete themes by giving you a red "delete" link next to each theme (see image below.) As we learned at the very beginning of this book under "Roles", only users with Administrator level privileges have the ability to install, activate, and delete themes.

(As of WordPress 3.8) When logged in as an Administrator you can delete themes in the Themes screen (Appearance > Themes) by hovering over a theme's thumbnail image, clicking "Theme Details" and then clicking on the "delete" link in the bottom right corner. You will get a browser prompt saying "You are about to delete this theme 'Theme Name'…" Once you hit 'OK', it is gone from the list of available installed themes and deleted from your server.

If you have dozens or even a 100+ extra themes, you can open the "themes" folder on your server by using FTP or the web host cPanel and delete their folders. Be careful that you don't delete the folder for the theme you have activated! And never delete the "themes" folder.

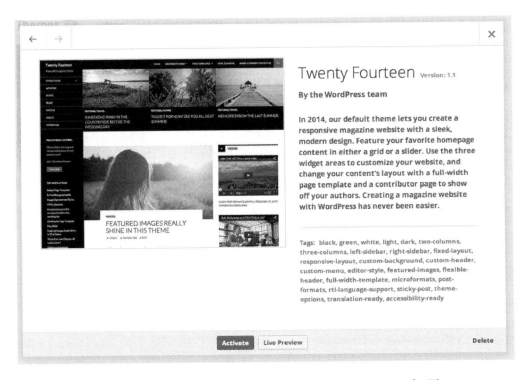

As of WordPress 3.8, in order to delete a theme you now have to open the Themes screen, hover over the theme thumbnail and click on "Theme Details" to see this modal window. Note red link in lower right corner.

When Should I Delete a Theme?

Here are a few common situations when you should delete a theme:

- it's broken or corrupt

- you are not planning to use it

- or you have switched away from it to a new theme and everything is going fine

Broken, corrupt themes

If you find you have a broken or corrupt theme (not one that was hacked and corrupted with malware, but one that is not working correctly and is displaying errors), you may want to stop using that theme. These themes can cause you trouble down the road by creating corrupted data in the database, missing data, or even errors that your visitors (and Google) can see.

Extra themes

As I mentioned in chapter 1A, some web hosts have a '1-click' or instant WordPress installer to help owners and operators install a fresh copy of WordPress in a few minutes. The problem I have found is that some web hosts are allowing this installation to also bundle a dozen, two dozen or even 100+ themes with your installation. It's the equivalent to buying a Windows PC and finding dozens of random apps and programs pre-installed that you will likely never use and didn't want.

Again, my advice is you only need two or three themes installed. If you end up with extra themes in your installation of WordPress, I recommend you delete them.

Don't know which folder is the active theme? There are two ways to find this out.

- One way is to look for the name of your active theme in the Themes screen (Appearance > Themes) and compare it to the folder names in the "themes" folder on your server. There should be one that is similarly named. Do NOT delete that folder.

- The other way is to visit your website (on your laptop) and right-click anywhere on the page. You should see an option for "View Page Source." This will bring up the source code for your website where you can do a search (cmd-f on Macs, ctrl-f on PCs) in this page to look for the word "/themes/" (yes, with the / on either side.) We are looking for a link with the theme folder name to be 100% sure of exactly which folder you do NOT want to delete—this is your active theme's folder name. So, you should (in most cases) find at least one line in the source code that looks like `/wp-content/themes/your-theme-name/filename`. Notice the part after `/themes/`, this is the name of the folder that contains your active theme. Do NOT delete that folder.

Switched, everything's good, and I want to get rid of the old theme

Ok, so you switched over to a new theme, tested the new theme (chapter 8), and you are happy with it. This is typically a time when people can't wait to delete their old theme, but unless the theme is corrupted with malware or backdoors I recommend you A) wait a couple weeks or a month to make sure there isn't an issue you missed during testing, or B) just keep it as your backup theme.

If that old theme is really making you upset that it is still around (it happens), then just give it at least a couple weeks to be sure everything with the new theme is okay before you delete the older one for good.

Pro Tip: Don't be too quick to delete an old theme that you once used. I recommend you use an FTP or file manager in cPanel to copy that old theme to your computer before you delete it. You never know when you may need or want it.

What Happens During the Deleting of a Theme?

There are two scenarios:

- one is the deleting of an inactive (installed) theme

- and the other is the deleting of an active theme—which you should never do, but can happen, so we'll talk about what actually happens

Caution: As of this writing, there is no "undo" button in WordPress like there is in Photoshop or Microsoft Word. In WordPress, to delete a theme or plugin means to delete it from the server. Content from Posts and Pages have a "trash" folder where deleted items are stored (for up to 30 days) should you need them again, but not themes or plugins. Once deleted, themes and plugins are gone for good.

Deleting an inactive (installed) theme

The big takeaway here is knowing what WordPress does when you click "delete." It really does delete the folder for that theme and its contents (such as fonts, background images, stylesheets, etc.) that came with the theme.

Once you hit 'OK' on the browser prompt the theme is gone. If you are backing up your website (which you should! See chapter 5), then a copy of your theme may still exist in your recent backups—if they were included as part of your backup plan. Deleting a theme from the Themes screen does not delete them from any backup files they exist in.

Deleting an active theme

Whoa. Please don't do this. But, let's say you logged into your server and did delete the active theme. Here's what happens.

Let's say you were in the cPanel's file manager and you accidentally deleted the theme folder for your active theme, or deleted enough of the theme's files that WordPress no longer recognizes it as a valid theme (see chapter 1B for what constitutes a valid theme). WordPress would then automatically select the default theme (if already installed) for your particular version of WordPress and make it active. Your visitors would then see this default theme instead.

Pro Tip: Always leave the default theme installed as your fallback theme. The reason for this is that WordPress will automatically activate it if your active theme gets deleted, goes missing or is considered "broken" because of missing files.

If you are missing the default theme, it will still try and load it as a placeholder, and your visitors will see a blank white page, or an error.

WordPress 3.6 and 3.7 use the "Twenty Thirteen" as the default theme, and 3.8 and 3.9 uses "Twenty Fourteen."

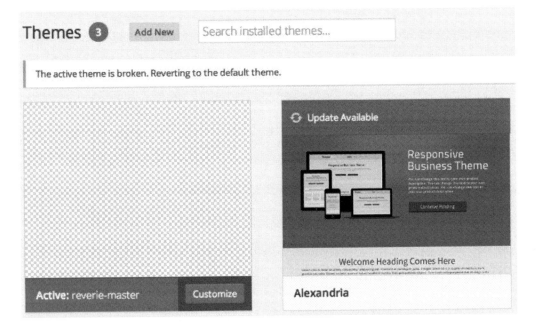

When the theme's folder goes missing or becomes renamed (for whatever reason) you may see this in the Themes screen. Note the missing theme thumbnail and the message at the top. In this case above, upon page refresh the default Twenty Fourteen theme was activated automatically since I had it installed.

After doing this you would have to reinstall the deleted theme and then reactivate it. That last part (activation) is important in that it isn't as easy as just quickly uploading a copy of the deleted theme to the themes folder. Should someone visit your site during the time the theme was missing, WordPress will look for the theme, see that it is missing/invalid, and rewrite the database (chapter 7) to use one of the default themes. If this happens, you will then need to log into the Admin Panel and activate the theme again in order to override the fallback theme.

WordPress is designed to fall back to using the default theme—if you have it installed—but I have seen cases where this did not happen. In some cases you may end up showing a blank white page to your visitors, or a big ol' error message saying there's a missing stylesheet. You know, it's best all around if you just don't delete active theme files. :)

What Doesn't Get Deleted?

Sadly, some themes can leave quite a mess behind. As we learned earlier, themes have options for backgrounds, font colors and so forth. The theme options are stored in your database. When a theme is deleted, that information remains in the database. If you decide later to reactivate that same theme, those backgrounds, font colors and whatnot will come back to life, just the way they were.

You might be saying, *So, my new theme will just use the background, font colors and other choices I made for my previous theme?* No, unfortunately not. Each theme stores its own options in the "wp_options" table of your database.

When you upgrade a theme to a new version it is using the same unique "option_id" (fields in the wp_options table) as its predecessor. Other themes that have their own unique option_id for things like font color will not pick up that color value from the database.

As stated earlier, anywhere your theme is backed up will not be deleted either. WordPress will not reach into a backup or anywhere outside the "themes" folder to delete theme files.

Pros and Cons of Deleting a Theme

Pros

- **It's safer** - Some old themes may have vulnerabilities in their code. Just because it isn't activated doesn't mean its files can't be accessed. The more old themes you have installed the more vulnerable your site is.

- **It's smaller** - Storing a bunch of themes that you will never use is only going to make your backups bigger and therefore take longer.

- **It's easier** - Managing the updates for a bunch of themes is a pain. Keeping it to only two to three themes makes this task easier.

Cons

- **Accidents happen** - I've gone and deleted the wrong theme by accident, and had to spend hours trying to find it again, download it, and reinstall it (it wasn't a common theme and stupidly wasn't in a backup.) In the early days, I once deleted the active theme while messing around on the server. Check twice; delete once.

- **Regrets happen** - Deleting a theme only to find later that, well, you can't find it anywhere on the web to download again (see above.) I recommend using FTP or cPanel file manager to copy your entire "themes" folder—or just a specific theme folder—to your local drive before deleting any themes.

Oh Crap, I Broke It.
(Installing the Backup)

For those of you using the self-hosted platform for WordPress, you have the ability to reinstall an older version of your entire website. This can come in handy for a variety of reasons.

Keep in mind that the below walk-throughs are what I do to investigate a site not working properly before resorting to doing an restore from my backup. There are probably a 1,001 things that can go wrong with a WordPress website, and this book cannot possibly cover them all. Nor is it meant to.

If you find you are having difficulty with your site, and do not feel comfortable doing the actions below or even restoring your site (and that's ok!), then I highly recommend you reach out to a WordPress professional. I also recommend that you move your site over to a managed web host such as WPEngine, LiquidWeb, or Synthesis, since this could happen again.

Wait! Do You Really Need to Do This?

Just because you think your website is broken and needs to be reverted back to a previous version doesn't mean you actually have to do so to "fix" it. Some problems are transient or temporary—clearing up in due time. You should consult the next chapter —"Shooting the Troubles"—to see if anything can be fixed in place instead of defaulting to the nuclear option of using the backup. To install a backup is to step back in time to the last backup, causing you to lose any data or changes you may have made in the interim.

How to Reinstall the Backup

While I have tried my best to be as thorough in my discussions of each topic I've covered to this point, on this topic I will have to defer to the backup service, plan, or plugin you have in place. Reinstalling a backup is outside the scope of this book. If you missed it, visit chapter 5, "Backing up your entire website", where I discuss your backup options.

There are hundreds of backup plans and services, and each stores backups in a different place/way, and each handles (or doesn't handle) reinstalling a backup in a different way. There is simply no easy way to go over this process in this book. I highly recommend you consult your backup service, plan, or plugin for details on how to reinstall the backup.

Beginner's Guide: How to Restore WordPress from Backup

I am going to defer to this great, detailed article by the website WPBeginner called "Beginner's Guide: How to Restore WordPress from Backup" found at http://www.wpbeginner.com/beginners-guide/beginners-guide-how-to-restore-wordpress-from-backup/

It covers the following topics in easy-to-follow language and pictures:

- Understanding backups and restoring WordPress

- Restoring WordPress using BackupBuddy backup file

- Restoring WordPress database backup using phpMyAdmin

- Restoring WordPress database backup using cPanel

- Manually restoring WordPress files using FTP

- Troubleshooting Backup Restore Issues

- Things to do after restoring your WordPress site

The one thing the article does't mention is that you can restore your database only, a specific folder only, or just the website files and not the database. If your site got infected with malware, then yes, you want to wipe it clean and restore from a *clean* backup. If you feel that you simply corrupted or messed up your database, then you can

176

blow away your database and restore it from a clean, known good version in a recent backup.

Your backup is typically one file (a .zip file.) But inside that .zip file is your database (a .sql file) and all of your website files (depending on what you choose to backup, this very well could be only your database. Check your backup settings for details.)

This means you can open the .zip and get the database file to use to restore your MySQL database. You don't always have to restore all the files, especially if you are sure that it is only the database that is having the issue.

What happens when you reinstall a backup?

Again, depending on the service, plan, or plugin you are using to backup your site, you may be able to reinstall part or all of your website.

Partial reinstall

A partial reinstall is typically where you are replacing a file, a folder of files (such as a theme), or even just the database.

Total reinstall - the "nuclear option"

A total reinstall should be your last resort. This effectively replaces everything: database, WordPress Core and all content.

When to Do a Restore

This is the tricky part, and when things go badly keeping a level head about the situation can help correct it faster. Here is what I do to check if the problem I am seeing requires a database restore or a full website restore from backup.

What happened just prior to the problem?

Did you just activate a plugin? Did you just upload a file or document? Did you just start a job/task via a plugin (such as a database or site wide scan, or another server-based job?) If so, let's focus on that for the moment:

- If your problem is showing an error message, copy and paste it to a text document immediately. Don't refresh the screen, you want to save this so you can do a web search for it. Also, WordPress error messages typically show/include the URL of the offending file, and in that URL is the plugin or file name. Really narrows down the search for the culprit.

- If there is no error message, and only a blank white screen, do a hard refresh (cmd-shift-r) while viewing it in your browser. Still white? Copy the URL from the browser address bar and open it in another browser (not another tab or window, but an entirely different browser.) Still white? Log into your cPanel or FTP and move your .htaccess file (found in the root of the website file structure) to your desktop. Make sure to delete the .htaccess file from the server, and refresh the browser. Still white? Place the .htaccess file back, as you may need to reinstall the database from a backup (see section above for link to article for instructions.)

- If the website takes forever to load just after you performed an action (such as a scan or backup), give it a minute (or five) to complete. Some services and tasks can task the processors in the server to the point where serving up your site takes a lot longer. This is common when using an inexpensive shared hosting plan (probably the most common web hosting plan on the planet) since they are often an economical setup and not the fastest server any hosting company has to offer. If the loading problem persists, the task may be stuck and in some cases a call to your web host may be needed to clear/stop the process.

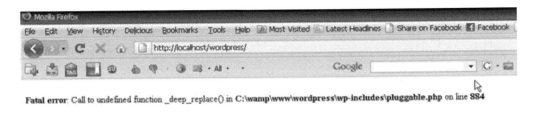

Screen capture from TechNama.com showing a "Fatal error." If this line appears instead of your website, it should be copied to a text document for further investigation. (Source: http://www.technama.com/2009/wordpress-fatal-error-call-to-undefined-function-_deep_replacepluggablephp-on-line-884/ June, 2014.)

Doesn't work, and you didn't do anything to it recently

If your site takes forever to load, or not at all, and you haven't done anything to it recently, a few common things may be at play: your internet connection is crapping out at that moment; the server your site is on is having issues; or your site is having issues.

- **Slow interwebs?** You can test your internet connection by trying to view another major site that you don't normally visit like Oprah.com. If it loads quickly, then your website's server may be experiencing problems or heavy traffic/usage. If all sites you view are loading slowly, your internet connection may be overloaded with traffic at that time.

- **Server down?** To check the server, look to your web hosting company's website for server status, or check their Twitter account for announcements. To find your web host's status page, do a web search for "[web host name] status" (without quotes), such as "Bluehost status", which happens to be https://www.bluehost.com/cgi/serverstatus/ .

- **Is it your site?** If the above two check out fine, it's likely your site. Call a friend and ask them to bring up your site. Not working for them? Move your .htaccess file to your computer and delete it from the server, like we did above. Still broken? In the browser window, look for an error message or any other indicator of the problem. If you have a recent backup, you can follow the article above to restore it.

Last Words

As I said in the beginning of this chapter, if you find you are having difficulty with your site, and do not feel comfortable doing the actions above or even restoring your site (and that's ok!), then I highly recommend you reach out to a WordPress professional. Troubleshooting and knowing when you need to restore from a backup is not always an easy thing to understand.

I know it's hard to see your site down—like seeing a sick child— but try and keep a calm head and investigate your site from many angles in different browsers on different internet connections. You may find that one of those combinations is the problem and not your site.

Shooting the Troubles

Know that we will only be covering theme-related troubleshooting in this book. And while I share some tutorials on how to fix a problem or two, this chapter is more about giving you the knowledge to investigate, research and possibly fix the problem yourself. Or at least be able to have a better conversation with a developer who can fix it.

.COM For those of you on the WordPress.com platform, know that you **cannot** do the following aspects of this chapter: create a development site, install plugins, update the WordPress Core, rollback a theme or WordPress Core. And you'll probably never have to worry about a failed WordPress Core update or failed theme update (and if they do happen, you would have the support of the WordPress team.)

Common WordPress Issues

For common issues and errors in self-hosted WordPress installations check out

- the WordPress.org Codex for troubleshooting: http://codex.wordpress.org/ Troubleshooting

- Hongkiat.com (pronounced hong-key-att) for the "10 Most Common WordPress Errors (With Solutions)," by Kay Tan: http://www.hongkiat.com/ blog/common-wordpress-errors-with-solutions/

- a web search for "common WordPress errors and solutions" (without the quotes.) Know that I will be covering tips on how to do better WordPress related web searches.

Hopefully problems are a rare occurrence, but I would be lying to say it will never happen. It will, so I'm presenting some basic troubleshooting techniques for common issues with themes. If you get queazy at the thought of digging in deep with your website, don't worry. You don't have to actually perform these operations, but it is important you have a basic understanding of what a broken site looks like so you are able to have an informed conversation with the developer responsible for fixing it.

> **Back it up!** Depending on the problem, you won't always be able to back up your site before you start 'shooting the troubles.' But if you can, do it before you start following someone's tutorial on how to fix it, or you risk making things worse.

How Will I Know There Are Problems?

Errors, issues, problems… whatever you call them they can be sneaky little buggers like an isolated hiccup. On the other hand they can be loud and glaring "Hey, I'm an error!" messages printed across the screen. Knowing something is awry will, at times, rely heavily on you knowing what is considered good, or correct.

Your last known good configuration

I highly recommend having a baseline to compare your website to. That baseline is something we established in the "Setting the Baseline" section of chapter 8. There we compared our website to a *last known good configuration*: in this case, the developer's demo for the theme.

The point of that chapter was to set a baseline for what it looks like when your theme is working correctly, thus becoming your new last known good configuration. If you one day visit your "Contact Us" page and feel it looks a little wonky, you want to have something to compare it to.

I want to reiterate that: at first, the developer's demo is the last known good configuration. After you install and test the theme, and everything is good, that new installation becomes your last known good configuration. *That* is your baseline to compare to. (Again, review the last section in chapter 8.)

A better option: Use a "dev site." Many developers and site owners create a development website ("dev site" or "staging site") to use as a comparison to the production site (as well as a site to test things on.) It is typically an exact duplicate of the production site, but lives on its own domain (or subdomain.)

More importantly, the dev site is a completely separate and independent website in every way. If the production site has issues, you can go to the dev site to compare. Keep in mind that this can almost double your maintenance costs in that you have to maintain two websites in order to have a proper comparison.

I've heard of developers setting up a dev site using WordPress Multisite (or multisite feature), but I caution against this as an independent baseline. This setup is not as effective in that it uses the same WordPress Core and theme files for both production and development sites. If the WordPress Core or theme is causing the problem, it will likely show on both sites, thereby causing you to lose your baseline.

In short, whether your baseline is "I have a good memory" (not ideal), a set of screenshots (good enough), or a dev site (ideal), you need a point of comparison, a last known good configuration.

Basic Questions to Ask When You Find a Problem

When you find a problem, you need to figure out the extent of it, if it's transient (temporary), and if it's an edge case issue (something that only affects a very small group of users/situations) that you can live with.

- Is the problem happening to all pages, just a single page, or group of pages with a common feature? This can help narrow it down to a plugin, theme feature, widget, or some third-party feature like a Facebook widget.

- Did this problem happen right after you made a change to the site, added some content or updated a plugin/theme?

- Did you try refreshing the page? Be sure you clear the browser cache, or do a hard refresh (Learn how to do a hard refresh: http://en.wikipedia.org/wiki/

Wikipedia:Bypass_your_cache)

- Is it happening only in one browser? Test your website across major browsers such as Chrome, Firefox, Safari (Mac), and Internet Explorer (PC.) Not all browsers support all features of a website, and every browser will render your website slightly differently. If the problem only happens in one or two browsers, check the theme's marketing page to see if that browser (and that version) is supported.

Knowing the Ropes Saves Money and Time

Knowing how your website is put together can save you countless hours in troubleshooting.

Think about your setup

Before you dive in to find the problem, you need to know at least the basics of your setup. For example, if you find your site is no longer sending backup files to your Dropbox account, you start with what is in charge of the backups: a plugin, your web host, or a third-party service (see chapter 5.) If you don't know how your site is being backed up, then you will likely spend a good portion of your time just figuring that out so you can begin to root out the problem.

The main reason I have people go through the tedious process of testing their installation in chapter 8 is to know your setup—knowing not only where the knobs and levers are, but what happens when you turn and pull on them. This is not much different than knowing where the fuse box is in your home, as well as having a description of what each breaker/fuse in that box controls. When the sparks are flying, flipping switches to see what controls what might not be a good option in either scenario.

Take notes

It is good practice to keep a log of problems you have come across, as well as how you solved them (if you were able to.) This log is a great way for you to understand what happened, how it got fixed, and more importantly act as a future guide to fixing the problem should it arise again.

You may not be the only one working on this site. If you call in a professional to help with a problem, they likely don't know your setup. Being able to give them an overview, as well as list any relevant work that has been done on the site recently can save them from going in completely blind.

Sharing notes with those that are working on the site is really helpful. I like to create a shared document that we can all edit and refer to when things go wrong—Google Docs, Dropbox, or Box work great for this. I've had clients that were able to refer to this document and use my notes to fix the problem themselves in less time than it would have taken to email me about it.

Find a solution to your problem on your own

I think this is often the best way to go about fixing problems since it is often A) free, and B) sometimes faster than waiting for a reply from a developer, and C) very rewarding when you fix it yourself. That last one isn't some self-help mumbo-jumbo, but real sage advice for all owners and operators of WordPress sites. You'll be pretty stoked when you find you can fix something yourself.

There are two ways to find a solution: A) visit the support website for the developer, or B) do a web search. Keep in mind that doing a web search can be tricky since searching on Google for "common WordPress errors" brings up "common WordPress mistakes"—not the same thing.

For those problems where you know are attributed to a specific plugin or theme, be sure to visit the marketing page (or developer's website) of that plugin or theme first. There are often support options, or even an FAQ page there to help you. Be sure to read carefully: developers often have very specific ways of asking for help. Some will want you to use a specific forum, others prefer email, and a few may even list a phone number for you to call (though that's rare.)

You can often find a link to the developer's website next to the plugin or in the stylesheet header of the style.css file in your theme (we went over the stylesheet header in detail in chapter 8.)

☐	**Limit Login Attempts**	Limit rate of login attempts, including by way of cookies, for each IP.
	Deactivate I Edit	Version 1.7.1 I By Johan Eenfeldt I Visit plugin site
☐	**Simple Custom CSS**	The simple, solid way to add custom CSS to your WordPress website. Simple Custom CSS allows you to add your own styles or override
	Settings I Deactivate I Edit	the default CSS of a plugin or theme.
		Version 1.1.1 I By John Regan I Visit plugin site

Screen capture showing two plugins with the "Visit plugin site" link.

Tips for searching the web for solutions

- Know how to do a really good web search. Knowing when to use fewer words, quotes, Boolean operators, as well as search-engine specific helpers can be the difference between *searching* and *finding*. I highly recommend this page from Google for tips and tricks to searching smarter: https://www.google.com/insidesearch/tipstricks/all.html

- Add the word "WordPress" to your searches. Why? Some errors/problems also apply to other website platforms. Example: "WordPress password recovery not sending email" (without quotes)

- If you see an error message on your website, copy it and place it in quotes, then add WordPress to it. Example (error message in quotes with Boolean search operator + WordPress): *"Cannot modify header information" + WordPress*

- Try posing your problem as a question. This is not recommended when doing research, but seems to work well for WordPress problems because there are a gazillion forums and comments about WordPress out in the wild, and a lot of them often contain a question. Odds are that if you have a question someone else in the world has already asked it in a way that may be very similar to yours. Example (no quotes; punctuation is typically ignored): why is WordPress running so slow

- If you can already attribute the error or problem to a specific plugin or theme, and you are not getting answers from the developer, try adding the name to the search. You may find others have solved it. Example (quotes around the theme name): *"Awesome Theme" will not show slider on home page*

(Some) Problems with Themes

While it is near impossible to cover every potential theme problem and explore their respective solutions here, I will cover some of the common issues that I wasn't easily able to find answers for.

Plugins vs theme

I've come across a couple theme updates that wreaked havoc on a website. In one case the theme update did not play well with a particularly aggressive caching plugin, and in another case the theme update conflicted with the jQuery already being loaded, which caused a slider plugin to not work. In cases like these, you have to make a decision to rollback the theme to a previous version or you could choose not to use the plugin.

While developers' intentions are to have their themes work with all plugins (and vice versa), there is no way for them to test every possible combination out there. If you come across a problem, be sure to notify the theme developer and let them know the details of your setup (WordPress version, full list of plugins, and theme version number) so that they can be made aware of the issue you are having.

WordPress Core updates

I had one client with a premium theme that relied on drag & drop editors for the Page and Post content. It worked well at first, but after a couple WordPress Core updates we found that the drag & drop editors were completely unresponsive and unusable.

This can happen when the theme's JavaScript is written for an older version of jQuery, and a WordPress Core update uses a newer version. This deprecated code can lead to hidden problems, as well as major meltdowns (depending on how much and what part of your theme is depending on JavaScript to run.)

If you update WordPress Core and notice things on your website behaving badly or missing functionality, check the Theme screen in your AdminPanel (or the theme marketing page) for an update to your theme.

If you update to the latest version for your theme and you are still having issues, try the half-splitting technique found on the "How can I tell if it is a plugin messing things up?" section of the FAQs in this book. Sometimes a plugin may be to blame.

The new theme ate parts of the website. WTF?

I had a client tell me that the latest theme update deleted ("ate") parts of her website. Long story short: the theme she was using had a lot of customizations to it that she and I didn't know about. When I told her to update the theme it overwrote those customizations.

The fix was that I had to open up her recent backup file to extract the previous theme files so that I could create a Child theme. Just another reason to use a backup.

Home page is broken (doesn't look like the demo.)

This will happen almost every time you install some super-tricked-out premium theme from a major marketplace. With these themes, many home pages require some major effort to get working properly, or even come close to what the demo showed it can do.

The fix is to consult the documentation/instructions that came with the theme. If you lost them, you will need to visit the the theme's marketing page to download them again. (If you don't know where the theme originated from, you can consult chapter 8 on how to find the marketing page again.)

Beware that theme documentation can be a mixed bag from amazing and detailed, to downright horrible or missing altogether. But, in most cases documentation should cover how to set up the home page. If not, reach out to the theme developer.

Rolling Back to a Previous Version of the Theme

If you find that a recent theme update is causing problems, you may want to roll back to the previous version you had activated. Since WordPress Core overwrites your old theme with the new theme, you are not able to simply revert to the previous one.

But, since you listened to me about backing up your site before updating themes and plugins, you will have a copy of it in your backup.

> **Where to find your theme in the backup:** Since there are numerous ways to backup your website, I cannot go over every one of them to tell you how to find your backup files. Some store it in a .zip file you can download, and others store them offsite. Consult your backup service/plugin for details on how you can access your backup.
>
> What I can speak to is that if you back up your entire WordPress Core, you can always find your theme by opening the backup file and looking for the "wp-content" folder, and then the "themes" folder. Inside that is your theme folder, usually named the same as your theme name.

If you didn't backup your website, you will need to get the previous version from the developer/marketplace. (If you don't know where the theme originated from, you can consult chapter 8 on how to find the marketing page again.)

If you refuse to backup your website, at least download the theme folder to your computer (via FTP or cPanel) before you update it so that you have a copy of the previous working version.

How to manually roll back a theme

CAUTION: What you are about to do comes with certain risks, and may not resolve your problems, and in a handful of cases may cause even more problems. The principle idea is that we are replacing the new theme with an older version (a process called a rollback.) This should be considered a last-ditch effort in troubleshooting, or when told to do so by your theme developer.

In nearly all cases that I have performed a manual rollback, I have found WordPress pretty good at restoring all my widgets and settings for the theme. WordPress works off of the theme's folder name, not the version number. So, as long as you are dealing with the same exact folder name, you should see widgets and settings come back to life after you re-activate the theme.

Rolling back a theme requires you to use another theme during the procedure. You will need to have the older version on hand and install it via the Appearance > Themes > Add Theme button in the Admin, or upload via FTP. If you are unfamiliar with a manual install, we'll go over how I prefer to do this below. There are a few different ways, but this one works best for me.

Quick, like a bunny! You should read through these 8 steps before starting and be prepared to do this in quick succession so as to minimize your visitors having to view your site while it is using a different theme. Also, be sure to do this late at night or during off-peak times—also to minimize the amount of visitors having to see the alternate theme.

1) Download from the developer or marketplace the version of the theme you want to rollback to, or download your backup file. Again, this should be the exact same theme, just an earlier version you know worked.

3) Backup your entire website.

4) Activate another theme from your list of installed themes: Appearance > Themes. Don't worry about setting it up; it will only live for a very short time. Hit "Activate" and go to step 5…

5) Using your web host's cPanel file manager (or FTP) navigate to the "../wp-content/themes/" folder and note the folder name of your theme and compare it to the folder name for the theme you intend to switch it out with. They

should be identical. Now delete the offending theme's folder from the server. Do not delete the "../wp-content/themes/" folder! That would be bad.

6) Once the folder is completely deleted, upload the older version theme folder to your server using cPanel or FTP. Its folder should already have the exact same name as the folder you just deleted. If not, you may have the wrong theme.

7) Go to Appearance > Themes and activate the theme you just uploaded. You should now see the theme in your Themes screen showing the older version number.

8) Check your site. Is it all working as it did before the latest update 'broke' it?

What to watch for in a rollback:

- In most cases, your Widgets should remain untouched once you reactivate the updated theme. They will likely be sent to the inactive widgets area (in Appearance > Widgets) during the process, but once WordPress Core sees the theme is back in action, it should reinstate them just as they were. Worse case is that you will have to manually drag them from the inactive widgets area and drop them back into their respective widget areas.

- You will need to check the entire site to ensure all your sidebars and widgets and shortcodes are working as they were before. This assumes you knew what your site looked like before, of course.

Use a plugin to rollback a theme

You can also use a plugin called "Easy Theme and Plugin Upgrades" to take care of rolling back a theme manually. It saves the current theme in a .zip file to your Media Library, uploads the old version and BOOM! you're done. Probably one of the easiest ways to do a 'manual rollback.' Watch for the same things as listed above. And always backup your site before you do this.

"Theme Install Failed" Messages

This message comes up when you are uploading a theme to your website via the Themes Upload screen (Appearance > Themes > Add New button > Upload link) and WordPress Core does not recognize it as a valid theme.

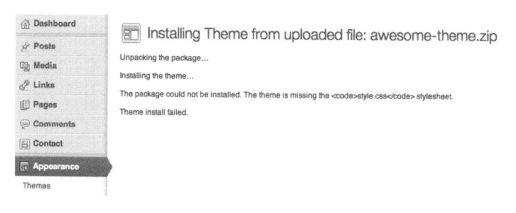

There are a couple reasons for this...

It's not actually a theme

You may be uploading the wrong file. This was covered in the beginning of chapter 6 where we went over all the extra stuff some developers/marketplaces roll up into the theme package. You may need to unzip the theme package you tried to upload to see if the actual theme package is deeper inside. It's not uncommon to see a folder called "theme" with a .zip file inside it that you are supposed to upload.

If you are still having issues, make sure you are uploading a .zip file that contains the style.css and index.php files in the root (not in a folder within the folder.)

WordPress simply requires a properly formatted style.css and a file named index.php in order to consider it a valid theme (see chapter 1B for valid themes.)

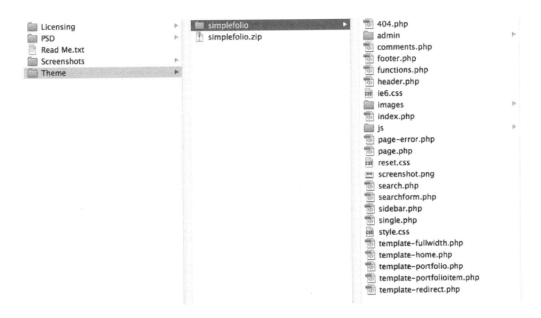

A screen capture showing the contents of a typical theme package. In this example, you would upload the "simplefolio.zip" file that you see in the middle column. The blue highlighted folder is simply the .zip file unzipped.

Missing pieces

As in the first image above, we see that WordPress is telling us what is missing: the style.css file. If you have the style.css file but are missing the header in that file, it will alert you to that fact by showing an error: "doesn't contain a valid theme header." If the upload is missing the index.php, it will throw an error stating it is missing.

These error messages should guide you to what is wrong or missing in the theme you are uploading. Open the .zip file you are uploading and look for the style.css and index.php files.

The empty theme: Strange as it sounds, WordPress is only looking for three things to consider it a valid theme that you can activate: 1) the style.css file, 2) the style.css header, and 3) a file named index.php. Note that the index.php file can be blank, it's just looking for the filename.

But, if the index.php is blank (which it shouldn't be), it will only show a blank page to your visitors. The takeaway is that WordPress is only scanning the uploaded theme for those three specific things in order to allow it to be a valid theme you can activate.

If you are having issues with WordPress accepting your upload as a theme, check the three things listed above. (You can review the details of a valid theme in chapter 1B.) If you find that the theme is missing one or all of these key components, contact the theme developer.

WordPress Update Problems

WordPress Core routinely gets updated to patch security holes and to add features. At the time of this writing, the most recent major update was going from version 3.8 to 3.9, with 4.0 scheduled for release in a month (August 2014.) When updates take place, your Admin Panel will display a yellow notification bar at the top of the screen with an update link recommending you install the latest version.

It's a simple two-click process that usually happens without issues. But not always…

Out of the hundreds of WordPress Core updates I have performed, a few have gone badly. In only one case did I have to reinstall the entire site from a backup that I created moments before the update. In another case the theme was very old (possibly poorly coded) and a couple features simply no longer worked with the new WordPress Core.

You may also get a notice from your theme developer/marketplace asking you to hold off on updating the WordPress Core. They may have found their themes to not be 100% compatible and are working on verifying and updating them. Just another reason you want to work with a developer/marketplace that actively maintains their themes and notifies you about updates.

> **Auto-updating.** WordPress has moved to an auto-updating model, much the way iPhones can auto-update their apps. By default, only minor updates (3.9.0 to 3.9.1) are being updated automatically, but you can have your developer configure your site to do major updates (3.9 to 4.0) too. Read more here: http://codex.wordpress.org/Configuring_Automatic_Background_Updates

IMPORTANT NOTICE ABOUT WORDPRESS 3.6

Listed themes are now compatible with WordPress 3.6. Please make sure you've installed most recent version of the theme if you're planning to upgrade to WordPress 3.6.

RT–Theme 17 version 2.6 released aug 07, 2013
RT–Theme 16 version 2.3 released aug 07, 2013
RT–Theme 15 version 2.2 released aug 07, 2013
RT–Theme 14 version 1.6 released aug 18, 2013
RT–Theme 13 version 2.4 released aug 18, 2013
RT–Theme 12 version 2.3 released aug 18, 2013
RT–Theme 11 version 1.4 released sep 4, 2013
RT–Theme 10 version 1.5 released sep 4, 2013
RT–Theme 9 version 2.4 released sep 4, 2013

Screen capture from the RT Themes' support website (http://support-rt.com/) as of Sep 21, 2013 showing themes that at the time were "compatible with WordPress 3.6" (meaning some were not.)

Rolling back your WordPress Core

Rolling back a WordPress Core update will take your entire website offline during the procedure. For a few mins (give or take) your visitors may experience a blank white page or a PHP error when viewing your site. **Be sure to read all the following steps before you start.**

> **Pro Tip:** before you run the WordPress update, always write down what version you are updating from.

CAUTION: What you are about to do comes with certain risks, and may not resolve your problems, and in some cases may cause even more problems. The principle idea is that we are replacing the new WordPress Core update with an older version (a process called a rollback.) This should be considered a last-ditch effort in troubleshooting.

In nearly all cases that I have performed a manual rollback, I have found WordPress simply wanted me to "update the database" to complete the rollback. This is a simple one-click operation that is presented to you by the Admin Panel (you can't miss it since this step, if required, takes over the whole screen.) In a couple situations, I had to use the backup to restore the Core and database.

1)   Backup your entire site.

2)   Visit the WordPress Release Archive (http://wordpress.org/download/release-archive/) and download the last stable version you had installed. Unzip the download package.

3)   Access your server via FTP or cPanel's File Manager. Navigate to where your WordPress Core is installed. This may be in the root, a sub folder, or subdomain. Don't guess! Make sure you are in the right place. As they say: check twice, overwrite once.

4)   Go to the WordPress Core you just downloaded to your computer in step 2. Delete the "wp-content" folder—you do **NOT** want to overwrite this folder on the server. Make sure there is no file called "wp-config.php" in your download. There shouldn't be, but check anyway—you do **NOT** want to overwrite this file on the server.

5)   Ready for it to get real? Overwrite the WordPress Core files on the server by uploading your local copy (minus the wp-contents folder and wp-config.php file) via cPanel File Manager or FTP.

6)   Wait for the FTP application or cPanel to notify you that all files have been uploaded and it is complete. Once it is complete, go back to the Admin Panel (you may have to log in.) You should/could get a full-screen sized prompt to update your database. Do it.

7)   Once updated, check the version number against the one you wrote down. Is it the same or a previous version? If it's the same, you uploaded the wrong Core,

or your database didn't update properly. Go back to step 2 and try again. If it is the version you intended to have, check your website for problems.

If this does not work, or makes things worse, use your backup to roll your website (including database) to the previous version. You did do a backup right before you updated WordPress, right? Get in the habit!

It's Probably the Browser

Let's say you are over at a friend or colleague's house and showing off your website on their computer. You notice that the layout of your site is showing page elements as having shifted around: what was once side by side is now on top of each other. WTF? Stop and review the section at the beginning of this chapter: "Basic questions to ask when you find a problem."

When you have visitors viewing your site with an old, outdated web browser like Internet Explorer 6, 7 or 8, they will likely see page layouts that shift around and experience other functional issues. Sometimes this can happen when viewing it on a smartphone (not the same as "responsive design.") Know that not all themes support these browsers and devices.

When a visitor tells you their experience with your site is problematic, ask them:

1) for a screen capture of the problem (if it's a visual problem), or at least a good description of what is wonky

2) what browser and version they are using (IE 11, Firefox 24.0, Chrome, Safari 6.1.1, etc)

3) what platform or device they are viewing it on (iPhone, Android, tablet, Mac, PC, etc.)

> **Pro Tip:** if you are finding it difficult to assess what browser you are using, visit http://www.whatismybrowser.com/ to get an immediate breakdown of your information, or have your client/customer do this and email it to you. You can then email it to your developer, if needed.

When you have that information, check your theme's marketing page (or theme documentation) to see if that browser and device is supported. Keep in mind that most themes sold today only support Internet Explorer 9 and above, though some have started dropping support for 9, as well.

FAQs - Frequently Asked Questions

Below you will find the most common theme questions I have been asked over the years.

Old Themes

I no longer get support for my theme. What can I do?

Meaning, A) the developer has overtly stated they are no longer supporting the theme, or B) they have fallen off the map and you cannot get in contact with them. You can either keep the theme you have, start looking for a new one (see chapter 2), or hire a theme developer to work on and maintain the theme for you.

If you are having issues with your current theme, buying a new one may not always be the best option. Consider getting a quote from a reputable WordPress theme developer to fix it. It may be an easy fix (and might not be a problem with the theme.) Also know that working on someone else's theme is not high on a developer's list of favorite things to do—it's someone else's mess, after all.

If you hate the theme you have anyway, then buying a new one via marketplace or theme developer looks like your best option.

> **Pro Tip:** I always recommend using a theme that has an active developer supporting it. Using an abandoned theme is not a good situation to be in for the long term.

How long do themes last?

Depending on how the theme was built it could be a useful, fully-functioning theme for a few months to a few years or longer. Themes are dependent on the WordPress Core, and when that gets updated some functionality of a theme may break (show an error) or parts of the theme may just fail to load. In some cases, old themes may have vulnerabilities such as outdated TimThumb.php code (see chapter 10 "Theme Maintenance".)

Themes that are actively being maintained by a developer could theoretically last indefinitely through updates. But, in reality, as we make advancements in HTML, CSS, PHP and jQuery, some themes may need a lot of refactoring to keep up. If you buy a marketplace theme with good support, this can typically be taken care of by making sure your theme updates are installed (again, see chapter 10 "Theme Maintenance.")

Full-custom themes will likely need periodic updating by the original developer, or one that doesn't mind working in someone else's code. Note that these periodic updates to custom themes will often come at an additional charge from the developer.

New Themes

Why doesn't the latest theme update look like the old version?

This depends on what was updated or upgraded in the new theme version. You should look to the theme's marketing pages for something called a "change log" or version history which will give you details on what changed in the latest version.

Let's say you see that the header is now twice as tall as it was before:

1. First, look to the latest demo or preview of the theme on the marketing pages to compare. Does it look like yours? If not…

2. Look for mention of that change in the change log. Don't see it? Then…

3. Log into your Admin Panel and navigate to your theme's options screen, if it has one. We are looking for something called "custom CSS." Look to see if there are any rules (CSS code) in this box that may be overriding this style. Don't have this box, or it's empty? Now is when you should reach out to the developer to see why this has changed.

If the demo or the change log show that this new look is part of the update, then you either have to live with it or customize the theme (which we discuss the principles of modifying a theme in chapter 11.)

Why am I missing things in the new theme?

This can go a couple ways: one is that you are missing things you once had before, and the other is that you are missing things promised by the developer/marketplace.

When switching to a new theme it is common to be missing things that you once had before. I recommend you read chapter 12 to gain a better understanding of what you can expect from switching themes. This can help you get an understanding of why you are no longer seeing a widget, a Twitter feed, or some other page element.

As for things missing that the developer/marketplace promised, you will have to take the following actions:

1) Open and review the documentation that came with the theme. Does it mention how to setup the functionality that is missing?

2) If it isn't mentioned in the documentation, or no documentation was delivered with the theme, check the marketing page for details on what functionality was to be delivered with the theme.

3) If you find that it is mentioned in the documentation or marketing page details, but still is not part of your theme, look for support help from the developer/ marketplace. Some have a forum where users can read past problems, current issues, and ask new ones. I highly recommend you search through these for your problem first, you may find a solution quicker that way.

4) If no forum is available, or you search the forum and can find no answer, then ask the theme developer for help.

I know this seems like a lot of work when you can just post a question or email them, but I assure you that on average you will find the answer quicker this way. Plus, the less you rely on developers the stronger you become for having resolved the issue yourself using the many resources available to you.

How can I install a theme update as a new, separate theme without overwriting the old theme?

I never understood why people wanted to do this, but I have been asked this a few times. I figured you could just change the name, but I needed to test it. It gets a little complicated when we get to the whole folder-inside-a-zip-file thing, so I'll try and explain that first:

If you take a group of files and compress them into a .zip file, the zip file will have a name given to it by the operating system (Macs use "Archive.zip" to name a group of files.) When you unzip "Archive.zip" it will create a folder called "Archive" so as to not drop a bunch of files all over the place (even if you didn't start with a folder called "Archive.") Let's say you renamed Archive.zip file to "awesome_theme.zip." When you unzip "awesome_theme.zip" it will automatically create a folder called "awesome_theme".

If you take a single folder named "awesome_theme" and compress it into a .zip, it will name the .zip file "awesome_theme.zip." When you open the .zip file it will create a folder named "awesome_theme." If you were to change the name of the .zip file from "awesome_theme.zip" to "test.zip", you would still get a folder called named "awesome_theme" when you unzipped it.

Got it? It's important to get that straight for when you go to create .zip files to upload.

Common usage: WordPress (and some other theme developers) wrap their themes files in a folder with a specific name they use for all versions, like "twentytwelve." When they zip that folder up, they often rename the .zip file to show what version it is, such as "twentyeleven.1.6.zip." So, the .zip file has a folder inside it that contains the theme files.

In short: Compress loose files and the zip file will uncompress to make a folder based on the zip file's current name. Compress a folder, and no matter what you change the .zip file's name to it will always uncompress showing the original folder's name. WordPress is simply uncompressing the .zip file, so the name of the folder it creates is important and you want to control that for when you want to install an update as a separate theme.

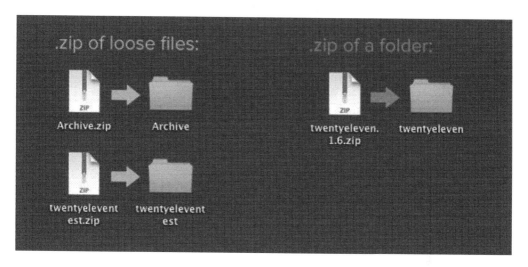

.zip of loose files:

Archive.zip → Archive

twentyelevent est.zip → twentyelevent est

.zip of a folder:

twentyeleven. 1.6.zip → twentyeleven

Test #1 - failed

1. I changed the theme's name by going into the style.css and changing the text listed in the "Theme Name:" part of the stylesheet header (very top.) In this case it was "Twenty Eleven", and I changed it to "Twenty Eleven Test". I then zipped up the theme files as "twentyeleven.zip."

2. I uploaded the .zip file via the Appearance > Themes > Install Themes > Upload screen, but after a few seconds it stated "Destination folder already exists. … Theme install failed." Ok, so the Theme Name attribute isn't enough to make it be seen as a new, separate theme.

3. I looked at the .zip file I am uploading and it is named "twentyeleven.zip", with no subfolder that contains the theme files. Like I said above, this last part is important: in this case WordPress will use the .zip file name to create a folder.

4. So, when WordPress unzips the file it creates a folder called "twentyeleven.", which (for this test) already exists in the theme folder. We cannot have two folders named the same thing, WordPress stops you from overwriting the existing "twentyeleven" file.

5. I went one step further and tried uploading an update of the Twenty Twelve theme to see if WordPress would allow me to overwrite the old folder. I had Twenty Eleven version 1.5 installed and was uploading Twenty Eleven version 1.6 (that I downloaded from WordPres.org) as a new theme. WordPress stopped me and said "Destination folder already exists. … Theme install

failed."

Test #2 - worked!

1.   I changed the name of the .zip file from "twentyeleven.zip" to "twentyeleventest.zip" and uploaded it. It worked because when WordPress unzipped the file it created a folder called "twentyeleventest", which doesn't already exist.

2.   Now I have two 'Twenty Twelve' themes, one as version 1.5 and the other version 1.6.

3.   Interesting thing happened when I viewed the Themes screens: WordPress lists the theme name as "Twenty Eleven/twentyeleventest." Since the "Twenty Twelve" theme already exists in the database, WordPress keeps them separated by renaming it for the Themes screen.

The takeaway is that no matter how you created the .zip file, you have to make sure the folder WordPress is going to create when unzipping it is uniquely named and not the same as any other folder in the themes folder on your server.

Why not just FTP it to the server? Yep. That's how I would get around this whole mess. But, unfortunately not everyone is savvy in the ways of FTP or even using their cPanel file manager to simply upload a uniquely named folder to the wp-content/themes folder. This .zip guide is for people who only know how to use the WordPress Admin Panel to manage themes.

CAUTION: Know that widgets and Customize options don't traverse. When you have two of the same themes installed with different versions: widgets and some options in the Customize screen don't traverse when you switch to the new theme.

The database does, however, remember what settings you made for each theme, so you can switch back and forth easily and your settings will be restored for that theme.

You would think widgets would be version-agnostic since they are essentially the same theme structure and the widgetized areas would be the exact same too. Not so. I activated "twentyeleven" ver 1.5 and loaded up some non-default widgets in the sidebar. I then activated "twentyeleventest" ver 1.6 and the widgets were moved to the

"Inactive Widgets" area.

As for the Customize screen (Appearance > Customize), only the Layout, Link Color and Light/Dark options will traverse between the two themes when you switch them.

Shortcodes, plugins and content do traverse between the theme updates. As for shortcodes, as long as the theme is the same structure and still supporting them, they should work just fine. It's pretty odd and rare for a theme to come out with an update that drops support for shortcodes they supported in an earlier version.

Plugins are a no-brainer: they are independent of the theme and will remain active so long as there isn't some conflict with the theme.

Same goes for content: switching the theme to the other version should not drop support for any text, images, video and audio.

Pro-level geek stuff about names in the database: Since we learned in chapter 7's section "What happens during activation?" that when a theme is activated the database records the theme's folder name, we can't have two themes with the same name in there.

WordPress also records all installed themes in the `_site_transient_theme_roots` row of the `wp_options` table. Each installed theme is listed out here. After performing Test #2 above I looked at this row and saw "twentyeleven" and "twentyeleventest" listed in the `_site_transient_theme_roots` row.

I changed the name of the "twentyeleventest" theme folder to "twentyeleventest-2" and reloaded the Themes screen thinking the installed "twentyeleventest" theme would be broken. But, it now had the name "Twenty Eleven/twentyeleventest-2" and worked fine. The `_site_transient_theme_roots` row even updated automagically.

I edited the `_site_transient_theme_roots` row in phpMyAdmin to remove the appended "-2", but it wouldn't take: looks like it is built off of the existing folders. So, I manually deleted the "twentyeleventest-2" folder from the server and not only did it get removed from the Themes screen, but `_site_transient_theme_roots` was also updated.

So, you can edit the names of installed themes' folder names (NOT active ones!) without any problems. Editing an active theme folder name causes your site to only show a blank white page, or automatically switch to the WordPress default theme for your WordPress version.

Ok, enough of that uber-geek stuff…

Can I legally modify a new theme? Even if I bought it?

Yes, you can. The moment you download any WordPress theme or plugin you have the right to modify it any way you wish, even if you bought it. It's governed by the GNU General Public License (GPL), which is one of the most heated topics among WordPress developers and marketplaces. You can learn more by doing a web search for "WordPress GPL."

How many websites can I install a theme on?

As many as you want. BUT, you should check with your developer or marketplace first. This is where the GPL gets tricky for some.

Technically you can buy a theme and do anything you want with it. Ethics should stop people from undermining the developer that relies on your purchase for income. Meaning, don't be a jerk and buy one then turn around and install it on every one of your clients' websites without paying the developer for each installation.

Know that some theme and plugin developers have pricing models that allow you to pay for a "developer's license." This allows you to install it on numerous sites.

Lastly, it is possible for some themes and plugins to come with a license key upon purchase, requiring you to enter the key in the theme or plugin's Admin or Settings screen in order to release it from 'trial mode', or to get it to work at all. Depending on your agreement, this could keep you from installing it on multiple sites.

> **Agencies and developers.** If you are interested in managing and protecting your themes, plugins or software, check out Pippin's Plugins' "Software Licensing" for the Easy Digital Downloads storefront plugin: https://easydigitaldownloads.com/extensions/software-licensing/
>
> This is a great way to sell licenses for support on full versions of themes. When your theme gets updated to the next major version (1.0 to 2.0), your customers can buy a new license and simply download the upgrade.

Can I copy the theme a friend has?

Technically yes, but I recommend you purchase the theme from the developer or marketplace. If you are having trouble locating the theme, there are instructions in chapter 8 to help you find its marketing page.

I recommend you not copy their theme. The main reason is you have no idea where it's been. Really, you may be friends and all, but you have no idea if it's been modified, compromised, infected with malware, or full of Black Hat SEO linking to pharmaceutical or porn sites. Even if you say it's clean, you know all the files are there, and you even scanned the site with Sucuri.net, I still say that you should first put in some effort to buy the theme yourself—it's the right thing to do, especially since most themes are very affordable.

Custom Themes

How do I find a developer for a new custom theme?

Pretty much the same way you would find a financial planner, or CPA:

- How long have they been in business?

- Are they current on the latest code?

- Do you feel you can trust them with your information?

Obviously there is a lot more to it, but if you treat this search and interview process like you are hiring someone that is handling your money, you should do fine.

If you can find someone local that fits the bill, great, but know that you may have to look outside your city or state for an experienced theme developer you can work with. I recommend starting with a web search for "freelance WordPress theme developer" (without the quotes,) as well attending and asking around at your local WordCamp (http://central.wordcamp.org/.)

Blasting out on Twitter that you need a WordPress developer to help you is a bit like standing on a dark highway with a broken down car and waving frantically: it's a gamble on who you will get, so be very cautious of replies to that sort of thing.

Lastly, ask for recent, live examples of themes they have coded from scratch. Check them out on your desktop, tablet and smartphone to see how they hold up across different devices and browsers.

How do I find a developer to modify an existing custom theme?

Most tattoo artists and theme developers I know shy away from working on other peoples' work for a multitude of reasons. One is that you should first ask the original person that created it. If the original creator refuses, or is no longer reachable, then a different developer may consider taking it on.

The bigger issue with custom theme development is that the new developer will have to spend some time figuring out the mess the previous developer left behind. Well, it's not always a mess, but I can speak for myself that in my early days of theme development I may have made a few developers cringe and shake their fists at me. And we all have early days.

Depending on how much updating you want/need, having a new developer update a custom theme might be as much or more expensive than having them create a new custom theme for you. Keep in mind the expense of your time in switching over to the new theme, too (see chapter 12.)

Also, if you are only looking to add, remove or modify parts of your them, consider asking a new developer to quote you for creating a custom Child theme for your custom one. This may extend the life of your current theme and can save you a lot of hassle in switching over to a new one.

I Got Hacked!

My site has been hacked, can I just (re)upload a new theme?

No, you should NOT do anything. I seriously and highly recommend you have Sucuri.net clean up your website. They've cleaned up a few websites I know of in under a few hours*, and I highly recommend them.

In many cases, there will also be malicious code injected into the database and in other files outside the theme, so uploading a new theme will not remove any of that.

*Time it takes depends on many factors. Contact Sucuri for details.

My site has been hacked, can I just delete the infected files?

No, same reason as above. In many cases, there will also be malicious code injected into the database, so deleting and uploading new files will not remove any of that.

Also, when you delete certain files you run the risk of crashing your site, losing functionality, or disabling your current theme.

My site has been hacked, can I just install the backup?

Technically, that is what it is there for. But, how do you know that the backup isn't infected or compromised too? If your website gets hacked or infected with malware, and your backup plugin or service makes a copy of it, you are essentially just storing useless junk since you won't want to reinstall a compromised backup.

This is where a managed hosting plan or a backup service that scans your files for problems really comes in handy. But, not all of us can afford that for our sites. In the case where we don't have these services—only a recent backup—you may have to reinstall the latest backup and rescan the site using Sucuri.net's free online website scanner to see if it is compromised. I go over scanning your site in chapter 4.

If you have multiple backups, you may need to install them one at a time—from latest to oldest—rescanning your site each time until you get to the one that isn't compromised.

My preferred method: Another way is to download the backups and scan them using your computer's anti-virus program. This won't catch any of the hidden links to pharmaceutical or porn sites since they aren't malware, but it will catch known malware.

Easy cleanup. All of the above options could take you hours to perform, and possibly take your site offline during the process. This is why I cannot stress enough how easy it is to just have Sucuri.net clean up your site.

Cleanup prevention. The better way is to never have a problem in the first place, which is why I recommend using managed hosting that seriously understands WordPress. Companies like WP Engine, Synthesis and Page.ly (to name a few) have servers and teams that understand the needs of WordPress sites like no other.

And since WordPress sites are a giant (and sometimes easy) target for getting hacked, managed hosting often has extra security, automated backups and malware scans. Some will help cleanup your site before you even know there is a problem. Doesn't get much easier than that.

Backups

Is there an alternative to backing up your website?

There are alternatives like having a development site that is a copy of the production (live) site. This is technically not a backup so much as a spare that you can clone to your production site. Depending on when the last time you updated your development site to match your production site, you could be using a months-old copy of your site.

Using a development copy of a website should be a last resort when all else fails. Depending on how old it is, you will likely not have any of your recent comments or blog posts. This is no way to manage a website. I highly recommend using a reputable backup service. Don't gamble with your website; read chapter 5 for some options when it comes to backup plugins and services, as well as the pros and cons of each.

Plugins

I realize plugins are a bit off-topic, but they do cause problems that can be blamed on the theme. And this half-splitting technique has helped me narrow down plugins without having to turn them all off.

How can I tell if it is a plugin messing things up?

Things can get wonky immediately following activation of a plugin. It's not always the plugin's fault. I've seen some that just happened to expose other problems I never knew existed. In one case a plugin that added a widget to display my GitHub projects caused malformed and unused data to show in my Custom Fields. I cleaned up the database and it worked just fine.

This is why it is a good idea to activate only one plugin at a time, then check your site for issues. You can always deactivate that plugin to see if it was the cause. If the problem doesn't go away, it may not be that plugin causing it.

There will be times when you need to turn on and off plugins to troubleshoot problems such as conflicting with each other or the theme. Know that deactivating a plugin will not erase any data or settings (just be sure not to delete it since *that* may delete data and settings.) To test:

- Turn off plugins one at a time, checking the site/problem after each time you deactivate one. In this case, you deactivate one plugin, check live page having the problem. If it persists, then activate the plugin again. Repeat for next plugin on the list.

- *Half-splitting* is reserved for when you have a lot of plugins. This will temporarily disable any security plugins you have, so be quick about it, but thorough. You deactivate half of them to see which half the problem plugin(s) is in. Then keep splitting that half in half until you find the plugin or plugins giving you trouble. So, if you have 32 plugins you would deactivate the first 16, and check the problem. If it doesn't change, you activate them and deactivate the other 16. If the problem still persists, it may not be a plugin. If the problem went away, you need to activate half of the deactivated plugins (8 in this case), thus repeating the process until you narrow it down to one or two plugins.

- The nuclear option is not advised for live sites, but may prove necessary for some stubborn plugin conflicts. This is where you briefly turn off all plugins at the same time to see if the issue goes away. If the problem goes away, you can turn on the plugins one at a time while checking to see if it comes back. Or, if you have a lot of plugins you can turn half of them back on (half-splitting) to see which half the problem plugin is in, like we did above, only in reverse.

As a rule, you should not be storing deactivated plugins long term. There may be cases where you are comparing two similar plugins, but once you make a choice you really should delete any unused plugins. Know that in some cases plugins will clean up after themselves and delete any data or settings they stored in the database.

Glossary of Terms Used in This Book

Glossary definitions in technical manuals tend to be some of the driest, most underwhelming things on the planet. I find great value in learning industry terms, so I tried not to make these too boring. If you believe a definition I offer is incorrect or doesn't meet your needs or industry standards, let me know and I will look into modifying it in future versions if applicable.

Glossary

404 Error

This is a an error message sent from a server when it can't find a file that has been requested. An entire web page that is missing can result in a 404, as well as a missing image on a web page. It is important to know that a 404 states the server can be reached, just not that file. Kind of like when the 24-hour donut shop is out of cruellers —what a shame.

Accessible

This refers to web accessibility in that all users—those that are able and disabled—can use the website. Some may find it odd that a person who has lost their vision would still need to use the internet. But, in a world where more and more companies and government services are relying on websites to connect with their customers or constituents, we need to be inclusive and allow for everyone to be able to get the information they need.

Admin

When I mention "the Admin", I am talking about the person that has administrator level rights to your WordPress website. WordPress currently has five roles (with a sixth for Multisites) that have varying degrees of 'powers' and access to the site's Admin Panel. So, the Admin is a person that has a specific role, while the Admin Panel is…

Admin Panel (or Administration Screens)

Some people call this the dashboard. I feel this can be a little confusing to some users since there is a section of the Admin Panel that is labeled "Dashboard", and I have seen some confusion in the WordPress Support pages about that. So, I prefer Admin Panel to describe the part of your WordPress installation that you log into to add/edit Pages and Posts, themes, plugins and more.

Each subsection of it are "screens" by which you navigate using the left side navigation bar, and depending on your role, some parts of this area may not be visible/available to you. See http://codex.wordpress.org/Roles_and_Capabilities for a list of what certain users can see in the Admin Panel.

API (application programming interface)

You likely use an API about 10-1,000 times a day and not know it. An API is the connection between many of the apps on your smartphone or laptop and the server that sends them data. Twitter, Facebook, and Soundcloud—to name a few— use APIs to serve up your recent tweets, posts and music.

APIs are built into some plugins to be able to talk to a server and share information. At the time of this writing, 17 APIs are built into the WordPress Core.

We learned the power and reach of an API in the Summer of 2013 when Twitter updated their API to version 1.1: everyone's Twitter feed on WordPress sites went dark. Twitter plugin developers had to update their plugins, then you had to update the plugin in the Admin Panel, and then you had to re-authorize the plugin via Twitter. This was all to create a better 'handshake' between your WordPress site and Twitter so you could once again populate your feed on your site.

If the Twitter feed was embedded in the theme, you would have to update your entire theme in order to get your Twitter feed working again. APIs change/update over time, so it is a good idea to leave things that fetch data from third-parties (like Twitter, Instagram and Facebook) to the job of plugins, not be embedded in themes as an option or feature.

Automagically

I used to think this term was too cute to actually use, but when you witness something cool and complex 'just work', well, it fits. Typically applies to things that are automatic or dynamic, but not always since it can also be used for things that are user-initiated and return data or assets that seem to work like magic.

Can also be used when masking the fact that the person using the word doesn't fully grasp how it works either.

Child theme

I'm going to let these lines from the WordPress Codex explain it best: *"A WordPress child theme is a theme that inherits the functionality of another theme, called the parent theme, and allows you to modify, or add to, the functionality of that parent theme. A child theme is the safest and easiest way to modify an existing theme, whether you want to make a few tiny changes or extensive changes. Instead of modifying the theme files directly, you can create a child theme."* Source: http://codex.wordpress.org/Child_Themes

Clone

This is the equivalent of copy and paste. You can copy a folder of files and paste it elsewhere, ending up with an exact duplicate. You can clone the contents of a database by exporting it and importing it to a new database. In both examples you have two identical things.

CMS (content management system)

WordPress is a content management system. And it does just that: help you manage your content. The "content" in content management system pertains to text (copy), images, videos and documents (PDFs) you upload to your website. You manage this content by using the WordPress Admin Panel to write, edit, save and publish your work to web pages.

cPanel

A cPanel (a registered trademark of cPanel, Inc.) is a commercial application used by web hosts to help make management of your server easier. Most server functions can be controlled via command line interface where an engineer inputs commands using only text. The cPanel is a graphical user interface (GUI) with helpful text and buttons to allow for non-engineers to interface with the server's functions without having to learn dozens of text commands.

A cPanel is also a common term for 'control panel', and while not all web hosts have an actual cPanel brand interface, they often do have a control panel that does many of the same functions.

CSS and CSS3

Cascading style sheets (CSS) are the part of websites that tell the browser how to display the website. It controls hundreds of things from font color, font size to how wide your website is and if the text is centered.

Today, you will see numerous theme marketplaces mention "CSS3." This is the latest version of CSS, and comes with many advancements to make the web experience more interesting. The key takeaway here is that CSS2 was the standard since 1998 (with CSS3 formally hitting the streets about June of 2011), so any web browser made before June 2011 likely does not fully support CSS3. This means that some features of CSS3—such as media queries for allowing your website to be responsive—are not supported in browsers such as Internet Explorer 6, 7, and 8.

If visitors to your website are still using old versions of Internet Explorer (6, 7, and 8), then you may want to double-check the theme's marketing pages to see if it supports them. Keep in mind that a theme developer still supporting IE 6, 7 and 8 is going to be rare.

Demo (or preview)

A demo or preview is where the theme developer or marketplace set up a website for you to see the theme in action before you download it. Typically the site contains dummy content, but in some cases it is a live production site. In some really tricked out demos, you may even get to change the colors and try out other options available to the theme. I've even seen some that allow you to log into the demo and view the theme's custom Admin Panel.

In chapter 8, we use the demo as a "last known good configuration" to compare our installation of the theme.

For custom themes and some boilerplate themes, you may not have the opportunity to play with a live demo before ordering it. A developer creating a custom theme for you should be able to show you some live sites that they created recently before you get into an agreement. As for boilerplate themes, these are typically very minimal and stark starter templates that have little to no styling, so a demo is not always available. In this case, the look and feel is left up to those designing and developing the theme, so showing a demo is moot.

Deprecated

This is the term developers use for code (especially) that is no longer in use, is superseded by some new way of coding it, or something we simply should not be doing anymore because it is not being supported by modern browsers.

Developer

Technically this is anyone that writes code for websites, even if they just started learning how 5 minutes ago. But, for the scope of this book I am referring to a knowledgable person that has been doing this at a professional level, and definitely for more than 5 minutes.

While San Francisco and the surrounding Bay Area are well-known for attracting and hoarding developers of all kinds, this is certainly not the only place to find them. In fact, I have worked with developers around the globe from Russia, Romania, Canada, the Philippines, Japan, Bulgaria, Ireland, Mexico and more.

You can check out the WordCamp schedule for a quick look at just some of the many places around the world that WordPress developers and designers are congregating: http://central.wordcamp.org/schedule/

Developer web site

I go over this in "Production" below.

Embedded fonts (Google fonts, @font-face, and Cufon)

You may have heard of "web safe" fonts. If not, they are a list of fonts that were deemed safe to use in websites because the vast majority of visitors' computers had them installed by the manufacturer. Therefore, fonts such as Arial, Courier, Georgia and Times New Roman were safe choices for web designers and developers.

Thanks to JavaScript and CSS3, we now have the ability to embed fonts into websites. What this means is that we can now use JavaScript and or CSS3 to load a font file into the browser, whereas before we relied on the visitor's computer to have the file on hand. Once the font is loaded, the user will see it being used instead of any web-safe backup fonts we declared.

On theme marketing pages developers will mention them as "Google Fonts," "@font-face," or "Cufon fonts." You may also see something called "sIFR" (yes, with a lowercase "s"), but I see this less and less, so I think it is on its way out, if not gone altogether. At the moment, Google Fonts and the CSS3 @font-face rule is the most popular in themes.

Also see "icon fonts" below.

Exploit

I think the current definition in Wikipedia sums it up best: "a piece of software, a chunk of data, or sequence of commands that takes advantage of a bug, glitch or vulnerability in order to cause unintended or unanticipated [behavior] to occur on computer software, hardware, or something electronic (usually [computerized])." Source: http://en.wikipedia.org/wiki/Exploit_(computer_security)

Themes and plugins can have unintentional vulnerabilities that people can root out and exploit to gain access, post code to your files and more. This is the number one reason you must keep your themes and plugins up to date (taking into account that it is being actively supported.)

File manager

There are numerous file managers in the world of web and computing, but this book is mainly concerned with the file manager that is found in your cPanel or control panel. It works much the way any other file manager works, but controls the files on your server. If you have a self-hosted WordPress site, you can use the file manager to add or remove files from your WordPress Core, theme, and other folders.

Fork

To fork something is to copy it and modify it without the intention of merging your changes back into the original source code (though you can offer to, and is up to the original developer to accept the changes or not.)

Freemium

Freemium themes are just put out with the intent of you 'test driving' it. Meaning, the theme's functions are limited in scope, and eventually you will be asked or prompted to purchase the full version.

FTP (File Transfer Protocol)

Simply put, this is one way to transfer files from your computer to your server, and vice-versa. You can use desktop FTP applications such as FileZilla (Mac and PC) and Panic's Transmit (Mac), or there is even an add-on for Firefox called FireFTP.

While the WordPress Admin Panel has the ability to upload images, documents, audio, videos, themes and plugins, there may be a time when you need to add, remove or inspect files on your server without using the Admin Panel. FTP is direct access to all your files, while your Admin Panel has limited access to the files on your server (and for good reason!)

Hacker

The hackers you hear about in the news are also developers/engineers that write code, only they—the news outlets and some parts of our own industry—use that term to denote them as having gained entry into a website, database, server or other part of the internet illegally.

HTML and HTML5

When you see a website in a web browser the primary structure of what you see is made up of HyperText Markup Language (HTML.) Coupled with CSS (and sometimes JavaScript), these languages are what make up the websites you see. Think of HTML as a cardboard box with a gift inside, and CSS as the wrapping paper. You can still give that gift to someone without the wrapping paper just as you can still show a website without the CSS (it's just very plain looking.)

Same as CSS3 above, HTML5 is a recent revision to HTML, and not fully supported by older browsers. In fact (and I won't get into the hairy details) HTML5 is not officially "recommended" and developers around the world have just been using it like there is no tomorrow.

It works, and is still being worked on with new features being added all the time. But, know that you will want to double check with the theme developer to see what browsers your HTML5 theme supports. There are tons of JavaScript out there called shims and polyfills that help older browsers use HTML5 websites correctly, but not all developers do this because it is a lot more work to test across all those old browsers.

Know that Internet Explorer 6, 7, and 8 don't support HTML5 without a lot of hard work (and cursing) from the theme developer. IE 9 does poor/spotty support for HTML5.

> **Check it!** You can check how your favorite browser scores for supporting HTML5 by visiting the http://html5test.com/ website. Be sure to give it a minute to run the tests.

Icon fonts (or Glyphicons, or Halflings)

These are really related concepts in that they provide high resolution icons to meet the needs of the high resolution screens like Apple's Retina, Google's Chromebook Pixel, and others.

Icon fonts are vector icons converted into font files that are loaded into the browser like embedded fonts (see above.) They scale (resize) like fonts do, and always look super sharp. Glyphicons are a brand of monochromatic, high resolution icon that can be loaded as images or as font files. Halflings are half-sized Glyphicons.

Infected

An infected website means it has a virus, malware, or black hat SEO. Basically it is anything some jerk injected/added to your website that harms your visitors' computers, harms your page ranking (because Google blacklisted your infected site), or is even so simple as adding a bunch of hidden links on your site pointing to pharmaceutical or porn sites.

Local

When I say "local" it means on your laptop/desktop computer, or more specifically on the drive that can be placed in your hand. Could be an external hard drive plugged into your laptop. Either way, "local" is not on your server or in cloud storage.

Malware

TechTerms.com says it best: "Short for 'malicious software,' malware refers to software programs designed to damage or do other unwanted actions on a computer system." Also see "infected" above.

Marketing page/website

I mention marketing pages a lot. I am using this term to describe the web page(s) that are used to market and sell WordPress themes. They can be one page or more, and come in various levels of bullshit ranging from none at all, to overflowing with. Most tend to hover around the no-bullshit side of the spectrum.

Marketplace

A marketplace is where themes are collected and sold for download. Examples of marketplaces are ThemeForest, WooCommerce, and Mojo Themes.

The key takeaway here is that they often sell themes that they themselves did not build. They are essentially a reseller of themes, or an online market where developers can post their themes for sale.

Note: The theme developer is typically the one that supports the theme, not the marketplace. On ThemeForest you work directly with the developer or a forum to get your theme problems solved, not the staff of ThemeForest.

Microdata/microformats

You will likely hear these terms in conjunction with SEO since they are used to organize and describe the contents of a page. They are code that is not seen by the user, but is seen by the search engine's crawler/bot to help it index your site's content properly. One such use would be for a business address, phone number and hours of operation.

Migrate and migration

To migrate a website is to copy all files and database to a new location. You typically do this when you are moving from a development environment to a production one.

An amazing and detailed video tutorial on how to migrate your WordPress website can be found at eduChalk: http://educhalk.org/blog/how-to-move-wordpress-to-a-different-server-and-web-address/

Nav, or nav bar

Short for navigation.

Owners and operators

This is the owner of the website and the operator (which can be the person maintaining it, but more importantly is the person who has Admin-level access to the entire site.)

Plugin

A plugin (or plug-in) is a piece of code that adds functionality to the website. This functionality can be as simple as adding custom CSS, or a Twitter widget, or as complex as a whole online store.

For self-hosted websites WordPress makes adding plugins easy with their plugin marketplace and installation via the Admin Panel. WordPress.com users do not get to use plugins.

Production (website)

Production often refers to live, public-facing products, and in this case websites. Web developers often set up a development (or "staging") website while creating themes, setting up websites, and testing out new functionality. This can be hidden from public view since it is not meant for public consumption (and you certainly don't want search engines indexing it.)

When the development website is ready it can then be migrated to the production website. The development and production sites can be on completely separate domains, a subdomain, a sub folder, or even stored on a local drive. Both are, at times, mirror images of each other and completely independent in every way.

The main benefits for this type of setup are:

- You have a place to test out new themes and plugins.

- You have a website that you can use for comparison should things go wonky on your production site.

- You can redesign your entire website behind the scenes, and when it is ready, you can quickly migrate it over without your visitors having to see you working on it.

Push-button

Push-button functionality refers to the ability to simply push a button to get something done. Can be used for a multitude of situations, but in this case I am using it to describe how one click in the Admin Panel sets off a series of events that happen behind the scenes which would normally take a lot of time to do manually.

Refactoring

Martin Fowler says it best: "Refactoring is a disciplined technique for restructuring an existing body of code, altering its internal structure without changing its external behavior" Source: http://refactoring.com/

Responsive

Responsive web design is where the website resizes, reorganizes, and reshuffles the elements on the page so that the user has a better experience with the website while viewing it on smaller screens. This does not only happen for mobile devices, but can be useful for smaller screens like the MacBook Air.

To see this in action, visit http://www.sitepoint.com/ on your desktop browser. Now resize your browser window to see the site respond to the smaller sizes. View the same URL on your smartphone to see how it resizes to fit the small screen without you having to zoom in to read the text.

Rollback

This is a procedure that returns the theme, plugin or WordPress Core back to a previous version. At this time there is no native push-button way of reverting back a version, so you have to do it manually by overwriting the file of a theme, plugin or WordPress Core with an older version.

Rollback is to be used only when you feel that the current version of the theme, plugin or WordPress Core is causing serious problems. It should be a last-ditch effort in troubleshooting, not the first thing you do.

SEO (search engine optimization)

This is the act of describing and organizing your website so as to be properly indexed by Google, Yahoo, Bing and other web search engines.

The details of SEO are akin to reading tea leaves since no one outside a small group of employees at these companies knows how it works exactly. I'll say it again: no one knows, it's all guesswork. There are best practices and things that people have found over the years to work better than others, but once things work too well Google, Yahoo, Bing change the rules.

Think of SEO as a library, nice and organized with an index. You have written a book where the title is "Soup sandwiches" and the contents talk about fishing, and the cover has an image of a skateboarder. How is the librarian supposed to find a spot in the stacks for your book? What if they decide to file it under "cooking" because of the title alone? If your book had a title that matched the subject that matched the cover, then you would have no problem getting correctly cataloged in the library. In fact, it would take only a few minutes to do so instead of the hot mess you might have had before. That's SEO in a nutshell.

As it pertains to themes, this is one of the most overused and oversold marketing points there is. While the structure of the theme can affect SEO, it's the title of the pages, the content and the speed at which the pages load that affect SEO the most.

> **SEO you can take with you.** A big drawback to using the 'SEO' features in a theme is that when you switch themes, it's gone. Any SEO title or description customizations you made stay with the theme; you have to type it all in again. Just use the "SEO by Yoast" plugin. It's the best SEO plugin out there, does more than any theme's SEO can, and you'll take any and all SEO customizations with you no matter what theme you use.

Server

This is simply the computer that your web host company assigned to your web hosting account. In some cases it can be several computers, and some hosts offer to host your files redundantly in servers across the globe to make serving your site to global visitors much faster (since it is physically closer.)

In the vast majority of cases, your website is hosted on a single server in a datacenter located in the middle of nowhere. In the case where you may be using a content delivery network (multiple servers across the globe) you still technically only log into one of them and upload your files once, the system automatically takes care of duplicating it across all servers over a short period of time.

Before you go off and get yourself a new web host, make sure you get the right configuration. Read the short WordPress Requirements here: http://wordpress.org/about/requirements/

Slider

Also called a slideshow, carousel, image rotator, slide deck and on and on. They are the ubiquitous thing on home pages all across the web to show you 2, 3 or 15 (!) featured images that you can scroll through. I call them carousels in real life, but since the vast majority of WordPress theme developers and marketplaces like to call them sliders, I will continue with that in this book to help you out a bit.

Spinning rims

Lately I have been using the term *spinning rims* to imply something is over-the-top and unnecessary to the overall function of the website (if not downright detrimental to it.) If you haven't seen them or don't know what spinning rims are, just Google it.

Examples of spinning rims in themes today: having dozens upon dozens of background images to choose from; 300, no 500, no 600+ fonts to choose from!; drag & drop page builders; and (my least favorite) a 100+ shortcodes that will never transfer to another theme should you decide to switch.

Theme package (or theme bundle)

Theme packages are .zip files that include a theme, and sometimes secondary files like plugins and documentation, tertiary items like Photoshop files, and even non-related items like hidden system files (Mac's .dstore files) or GitHub files (usually .md and .gitignore files.)

When you do a search for a theme in the Appearance >Themes > Add New screen, you are only searching within the WordPress.org Theme Directory (a marketplace.) These .zip files download directly to your server and install automatically with no additional files (you won't even see the .zip file.) Though, you can find that theme in the WordPress.org Theme Directory (http://wordpress.org/themes/) and download the theme package to your computer, if you wish.

> **Protect yourself.** It's uncommon, but themes can come infected with malware, viruses and other harmful crap. Any theme you download to your computer should be scanned with your anti-virus program before installing, especially any full-featured themes that are free.
>
> Frankly, when I install directly via the Appearance >Themes > Add New screen from WordPress, I am assuming WordPress.org is scanning all themes in their Theme Directory for malware. If you still feel queazy about this, you can download the package directly from the Directory (http://wordpress.org/themes/) and scan it before installing it.
>
> The other way to protect yourself is to only deal with established and reputable marketplaces and developers. If the website is offering too-good-to-be-true themes for free, there might be something wrong.

Vulnerability

First thing is vulnerabilities are often unintentional. If it is intentional, we call it a backdoor or some other nefarious term. In nearly all cases these are simply weak spots in software that allow someone to exploit the system.

A widespread vulnerability was found in a piece of code called TimThumb. It resizes images for the website, and someone found out that it allowed a hacker or bot to upload code to the server by gaining access to this file. Finding the TimThumb file was easy once you knew where it was stored in a theme, and since some themes sold to tens of thousands of people, boom!, hackers and bots have access to tens of thousands of servers.

In the end, it is estimated that millions of websites were vulnerable to attack because of TimThumb image re-sizing. Just another reason to keep your themes and plugins up to date.

Web app

A web app is an application that is accessed via a web browser like Internet Explorer, Firefox, Chrome and others. This is similar to an app on your smartphone in that it is designed to allow you to interact with it to perform a set of functions and tasks. It is also very different from a smartphone app in that you do not have to download it in order to use it.

So, a web app interface is hosted on the company's server, while the smartphone app interface is hosted on your device. Both connect to a server that receives and understands your commands.

Other examples of web apps are GMail, Google Docs, MailChimp, Facebook, Twitter and the new Microsoft Outlook.

Web host

This is the company that owns and or operates the servers you store your website files on. Some notable ones for WordPress are HostGator, BlueHost, WPEngine, and Synthesis (with the last two names really focusing on hosting WordPress sites.)

In the cases of companies like HostGator and BlueHost you pay them to host files on the server and for the most part all the maintenance and problem solving is up to you. This is called self-hosting. They take care of the servers, and in the vast majority of cases will not be able to help you out with issues like getting malware off your website or even tuning the server for better performance.

Managed hosting is what WPEngine and Synthesis do. They actually manage several aspects of your WordPress installation, as well as protect it, scan for problems and tune their servers to specifically meet the needs of WordPress users. You can expect to pay more for managed hosting, of course.

Widgets

Widgets are areas on your website that you can insert content via the Appearance >

Widgets screen in the Admin Panel. It is common for these areas to be in a sidebar, but they can be in headers, footers, main content areas and elsewhere. Placement of them is up to the theme developer.

It is important to know that widgets are tied to the theme. Meaning, if your current theme has three widget areas in the sidebar, your new theme won't recognize them, even if it too has three areas for widgets in the sidebar. The reason is that the theme's widgets all have unique names assigned to them. It is highly unlikely that your new theme will have the exact same names for its widget areas.

Widgetize

Widgetize is a word that the WordPress community had to make up to cover the act of making a theme able to support widgets.

WordPress v. WordPress Core v. WordPress.org v. WordPress.com

I go over this in detail in the "Before we get started" chapter at the beginning of this book.

Resources

Throughout this book I mention articles, developers, marketplaces, services and more. Below you will find a list of those resources (in alphabetical order.)

A

AIGA's position on spec work (article): http://www.aiga.org/position-spec-work/

Akismet: http://akismet.com/

AVG anti-virus: http://free.avg.com/

AVAST anti-virus: http://www.avast.com/

B

BackupBuddy, by iThemes: http://ithemes.com/purchase/backupbuddy/

BackUpWordPress, by Human Made Limited: http://wordpress.org/plugins/backupwordpress/

Basis (boilerplate theme), by Josiah Spence — http://codecarpenter.com/freebie/basis-a-wordpress-boilerplate-theme/

bbPress: http://bbpress.org/

Bluehost (web host): http://www.bluehost.com/

Bluehost status page: https://www.bluehost.com/cgi/serverstatus/

Bones (boilerplate theme): http://themble.com/bones/

Brad Frost on carousels: http://bradfrostweb.com/blog/post/carousels/

C

Can I Use: http://caniuse.com/

Chrome (web browser): https://www.google.com/intl/en-US/chrome/browser/

CPanel: http://cpanel.net/

Cruz Skate Shop: http://cruzskateshop.com/

Cufon: http://cufon.shoqolate.com/generate/

D

Disable WordPress Theme Updates plugin: https://wordpress.org/plugins/disable-wordpress-theme-updates/

Drupal: https://drupal.org/

E

Easy Digital Downloads marketplace for themes: https://easydigitaldownloads.com/themes/

Easy Digital Downloads marketplace for plugins ("Extensions"): https://easydigitaldownloads.com/extensions/

Easy Digital Downloads plugin: https://easydigitaldownloads.com/

Easy Digital Downloads "Software Licensing" plugin: https://easydigitaldownloads.com/extensions/software-licensing/

Easy Theme and Plugin Upgrades plugin: https://wordpress.org/plugins/easy-theme-and-plugin-upgrades/

Edge Inspect App (by Adobe): http://html.adobe.com/edge/inspect/

EduChalk's how to migrate your WordPress website: http://educhalk.org/blog/how-to-move-wordpress-to-a-different-server-and-web-address/

Elegant Themes: http://www.elegantthemes.com/

Envato's ThemeForest: http://themeforest.net/

F
Facebook Open Graph: https://developers.facebook.com/docs/opengraph

Firefox (web browser): http://www.mozilla.org/en-US/firefox/new/

G
Genesis Framework: http://my.studiopress.com/themes/genesis/

Ghostlab App: http://vanamco.com/ghostlab/

GitHub: https://github.com/

GNU General Public License (GPL): http://www.gnu.org/copyleft/gpl.html

GoDaddy (web host): http://www.godaddy.com/

Google Analytics: http://www.google.com/analytics/

Google Drive: https://drive.google.com/

Google Fonts: https://www.google.com/fonts

Google's tips and tricks to searching smarter: https://www.google.com/insidesearch/tipstricks/all.html

Gumroad: https://gumroad.com/

H
Hide Unwanted Shortcodes plugin: http://wordpress.org/plugins/hide-unwanted-shortcodes/

Hide Broken Shortcodes plugin: http://wordpress.org/plugins/hide-broken-shortcodes/

Hongkiat's article "10 Most Common WordPress Errors (With Solutions)": http://

www.hongkiat.com/blog/common-wordpress-errors-with-solutions/

HostGator (web host): http://www.hostgator.com/

HostMonster (web host): http://www.hostmonster.com/

HTML5 Test: http://html5test.com/

I

InfinteWP: http://infinitewp.com/

Internet Explorer (web browser): http://windows.microsoft.com/en-us/internet-explorer/download-ie

Irex Lite (theme), by Tikendra Maitry: http://wordpress.org/themes/irex-lite

J

Jigoshop: http://jigoshop.com/

L

LESS (CSS preprocessor): http://lesscss.org/

LiquidWeb (managed web hosting): http://www.liquidweb.com/wordpress-hosting.html

M

MailChimp: http://mailchimp.com/

ManageWP, by ManageWP: https://managewp.com/

N

New York Times article on impatient users: http://www.nytimes.com/2012/03/01/technology/impatient-web-users-flee-slow-loading-sites.html

O

Omniture (Adobe Marketing Cloud): http://www.adobe.com/solutions/digital-marketing.html

Orbisius Broken Shortcode Checker plugin (premium): http://codecanyon.net/item/

orbisius-broken-shortcode-checker/3767488

P

Page.ly (managed web hosting): https://pagely.com/

Photoshop (by Adobe): http://www.photoshop.com/

Pippin's Pluggins: http://pippinsplugins.com/

Pippin Williamson article "Functionality: Plugins vs Themes": http://wp.tutsplus.com/articles/general/functionality-plugins-vs-themes/

R

RackSpace: http://www.rackspace.com/

Responsive (theme), by CyberChimps: http://wordpress.org/themes/responsive

Rodrigo Galindez (theme developer): http://www.rodrigogalindez.com/themes/modernist/

Roots (boilerplate theme), by Ben Word: http://roots.io/

RoyalSlider plugin: http://dimsemenov.com/plugins/royal-slider/wordpress/

S

Safari (web browser): https://www.apple.com/safari/

SaSS (CSS preprocessor): http://sass-lang.com/

Section 508 (accessibility standards in information technology): http://www.section508.gov/

Siemens carousel study: http://www.nngroup.com/articles/auto-forwarding/

Simple Admin Notes plugin: https://wordpress.org/plugins/simple-admin-notes/

Simple Custom CSS plugin: https://wordpress.org/plugins/simple-custom-css/

SimpleFolio theme): http://www.smashingmagazine.com/2010/02/07/simplefolio-a-free-clean-portfolio-wordpress-theme/

Sitepoint: http://www.sitepoint.com/

SiteVault: http://www.site-vault.com/

Skeleton (boilerplate theme): http://themes.simplethemes.com/skeleton/

Smashing Magazine (blog category "WordPress"): http://wp.smashingmagazine.com/

Soliloquy plugin: http://soliloquywp.com/

Sophos anti-virus: http://www.sophos.com/

Spun (theme), by Caroline Moore: http://wordpress.org/themes/spun

Sucuri: https://sucuri.net/

Sucuri article "Dissecting a WordPress Brute Force Attack": http://blog.sucuri.net/2013/07/dissecting-a-wordpress-brute-force-attack.html

Sucuri article "Timthumb.php Mass Infection – Aftermath – Part I": http://blog.sucuri.net/2011/10/timthumb-php-mass-infection-aftermath-part-i.html

Sucuri Security - SiteCheck Malware Scanner plugin: https://wordpress.org/plugins/sucuri-scanner/

Synthesis (managed web hosting): http://websynthesis.com/

T

Theme-Check plugin: https://wordpress.org/plugins/theme-check/

ThemeForest's "WordPress Theme Submission Requirements": http://support.envato.com/index.php?/Knowledgebase/Article/View/472

TimThumb image resized: http://www.binarymoon.co.uk/projects/timthumb/

TGM Plugin Activation class: http://tgmpluginactivation.com/

Torque Magazine blog: http://torquemag.io/

Twitter Cards: https://dev.twitter.com/docs/cards

Twitter Embeds: http://en.support.wordpress.com/twitter/twitter-embeds/

U

_S ("Underscores" theme), by Automattic — http://underscores.me/

University of Notre Dame carousel study: http://weedygarden.net/2013/01/carousel-stats/

V

VaultPress, by Automattic: http://vaultpress.com/

W

W3 Total Cache plugin: https://wordpress.org/plugins/w3-total-cache/

WeedyGarden.net carousel stats: http://weedygarden.net/2013/01/carousel-stats/

What is My Browser?: http://www.whatismybrowser.com/

Wikipedia, learn how to do a hard refresh: http://en.wikipedia.org/wiki/Wikipedia:Bypass_your_cache

WooCommerce: http://www.woothemes.com/woocommerce/

WooThemes: http://www.woothemes.com/

WordCamp: http://central.wordcamp.org/

WordPress.com

WordPress.com Stats: http://en.wordpress.com/stats/misc/

WordPress.org

WordPress Codex: http://codex.wordpress.org/

WordPress Codex, "Child Themes": http://codex.wordpress.org/Child_Themes

WordPress Codex, "Troubleshooting": http://codex.wordpress.org/Troubleshooting

WordPress Codex, "Using Themes": http://codex.wordpress.org/Using_Themes

WordPress Codex, "Validating a Website": http://codex.wordpress.org/Validating_a_Website

WordPress Core: https://wordpress.org/download/

WordPress Importer plugin: https://wordpress.org/plugins/wordpress-importer/

WordPress Loop: http://codex.wordpress.org/The_Loop_in_Action

WordPress.com Plans: http://store.wordpress.com/plans/

WordPress Plugins Directory: http://wordpress.org/plugins/

WordPress Release Archive: http://wordpress.org/download/release-archive/

WordPress Requirements: http://wordpress.org/about/requirements/

WordPress Theme Directory: http://wordpress.org/themes/

WordPress Theme Review: http://codex.wordpress.org/Theme_Review

WPBeginner article "Beginner's Guide: How to Restore WordPress from Backup": http://www.wpbeginner.com/beginners-guide/beginners-guide-how-to-restore-wordpress-from-backup/

WPEngine (managed web hosting): http://wpengine.com/

wpmudev article "Free WordPress Themes: The Ultimate Guide": http://premium.wpmudev.org/blog/free-wordpress-themes-ultimate-guide/

WPSecurityLock.com

WPSmith.net article "A Theme Framework, Child Themes, & Grandchild Themes": http://wpsmith.net/2014/wp/theme-framework-child-themes-grandchild-themes/

WP Tavern blog (tag "themes"): http://www.wptavern.com/tag/themes

Y

YIThemes: http://yithemes.com/

Yoast's WordPress SEO plugin: https://yoast.com/wordpress/plugins/seo/

Made in the USA
Middletown, DE
12 November 2018